T0355579

Visual Methods for Digital Research

Visual Methods for Digital Research

An Introduction

Sabine Niederer and Gabriele Colombo

polity

First published in 2024 by Polity Press

Polity Press
65 Bridge Street
Cambridge CB2 1UR, UK

Polity Press
111 River Street
Hoboken, NJ 07030, USA

ISBN-13: 978-1-5095-4254-3
ISBN-13: 978-1-5095-4255-0 (pb)

A catalogue record for this book is available from the British Library.

Library of Congress Control Number: 2023951948

Typeset in 10.5 on 12pt Sabon
by Fakenham Prepress Solutions, Fakenham, Norfolk NR21 8NL
Printed and bound in Great Britain by TJ Books Ltd, Padstow, Cornwall

The publisher has used its best endeavours to ensure that the URLs for external websites referred to in this book are correct and active at the time of going to press. However, the publisher has no responsibility for the websites and can make no guarantee that a site will remain live or that the content is or will remain appropriate.

Every effort has been made to trace all copyright holders, but if any have been overlooked the publisher will be pleased to include any necessary credits in any subsequent reprint or edition.

For further information on Polity, visit our website:
politybooks.com

Contents

Figures

Preface

In an age where images pervade our digital culture and shape societal discussions, the need to examine them critically has never been greater. The scholarship on visual methodologies has traditionally focused on studying images – their production, meaning, circulation, and reception – and their role as research tools. This book, *Visual Methods for Digital Research*, builds on the field of visual methodologies while focusing on the specificity of digital visual culture. It offers methods and approaches tailored for the researcher and student interested in contemporary digital visual culture. Each chapter starts with a vignette (an artwork or a picture depicting a particular research setting) that sets the tone for the themes discussed in the chapter.

For this preface, it seems only fitting to start with the cover of the book you hold in your hands. The cover image shows *Esercizio n.7 / Déjà vu* by artist Caterina Rossato: an assemblage of cut-out landscapes, neatly arranged one behind the other, is held together by two poster clips. The images combined create new and non-existent landscapes that yet seem familiar. Where are these mountains again? Didn't I swim in that cold lake? By layering and stacking, the landscapes become a collection of memories of mountains, canyons, forests, lakes, and buildings illuminated by rays of sunlight.

The work not only shows a collection of images, reassembled in this case to trigger the sense of déjà vu and play with false memories of landscapes visited. It also is a beautiful example of – to put it very simply – 'doing things' with images. In this book, we discuss methods for studying digital images that work with images by assembling them, re-displaying them, overlaying them, annotating them, talking to them, and so on. The cover image speaks to us as visual digital methods similarly involve creative ways to use images *as material*. Art and the realm of design are important sites of visual research, where – just as in visual digital research – the results often raise new questions. That is the excitement and inspiration we find in this field and the reason we draw in examples from the arts when discussing visual digital research.

In our research and teaching, we have increasingly turned our attention to the study of mostly visual materials. In 2019, we started to describe and publish some of the approaches for doing research with and about digital images with the international journal *Diseña*. In the issue dedicated to design methods, we outlined visual methodologies for collaborative research, cross-platform analysis, and public participation (Niederer & Colombo, 2019). A few years later, in the same journal, we curated a special issue dedicated to visual methods for online images (Colombo & Niederer, 2021), collecting a variety of research perspectives for approaching digital visual culture with visual methods.

This book is intended as a guide for researchers and students who share our interest in visual methods and may consider using them in their own digital research. It offers a range of approaches for interfacing online images that seek to understand, reanimate, republish, and change perspectives on our digital visual culture. It offers practical advice on how to use visual research methods effectively and provides examples of how (digital) visual research methods have been used in different research contexts. It is our hope that this book will inspire other researchers and students to consider the potential of visual research methods for their own practice.

Research considerations

While the book's primary focus is on studying images in groups, it does not overlook the importance of the single image. Drawing

0.1 *Esercizio n.7 / Déjà vu.* Caterina Rossato, 2014.

inspiration from canonical works on the subject, it advocates for a methodology that combines both distant and close reading. This dialectical approach echoes W. J. T. Mitchell's concept of the 'pictorial turn', highlighting how each image serves as a microcosm of cultural meaning that requires deep analysis. The theme of social and cultural relevance runs throughout the book. Most projects mentioned in the chapters lean heavily into issue mapping (Marres, 2015b) and controversy mapping, underscoring the societal impact and implications of the images under study.

Positioned firmly within the humanities, this book bridges the gap between theory and practice. It takes into account seminal works in visual communications and visual methodologies, incorporating perspectives from scholars such as Aiello and Parry, and Rose. The book serves as both a theoretical primer and a practical guide, offering a comprehensive framework enriched by compelling examples and hands-on techniques. Whether you're a student or an experienced researcher, this book aims to make the – sometimes complex – field of digital visual research more accessible.

This book does not offer chapters dedicated to the ethics of digital research or the critical assessment of the problematic hegemonic position of a handful of online platforms. Nonetheless, ethical considerations, particularly concerning whose images are studied and how, underpin the works presented in this book. Data feminism and the ethics of studying images that were not explicitly created for research purposes are discussed in various case studies. We encourage the readers of this book to think critically about the visual data they engage with and how to do so responsibly.

Another element that stands firmly behind the scenes consists of the ways of working: the practical aspects of doing digital research – which often takes place in group work, sprints, and collaborations. The book intentionally avoids extensive lists of tools, focusing instead on the conceptual underpinnings that can be applied across a variety of platforms and technologies. Rather than one-on-one *How-to*'s, we presented research protocols more like recipes, offering the reader a foundation upon which to improvise and innovate, and which they can adapt to their own research contexts.

In selecting the case studies, artworks, and scholarly references featured in this book, we have made a deliberate choice to draw upon our own academic and experiential backgrounds, with roots in the humanities and within a European setting of applied sciences (in Amsterdam, The Netherlands, and Milan, Italy, specifically). Our research contexts are also interwoven with highly collaborative practices of design as well as artistic and cultural research. As we present these examples, we aim to offer readers a window into the research settings that have informed our own work, paying testament to the people and settings that have shaped our perspectives and understanding of the field.

Then again, this book does not exist in a vacuum. It is in conversation with a vast and growing body of work in digital and visual methods, data feminism, and visual communications. If you have interests in these fields, this book serves as both an entry point and, hopefully, a catalyst for deeper exploration.

Outline of chapters

Chapter 1 discusses theorizations of the digital image. Through the critical analysis of art and design projects, we review different characterizations of digital images, including their materiality, networked nature, multiplicity, and circulation. We end the chapter with a review of different strategies for compiling collections of images.

In *chapter 2*, we detail various displaying formats and present strategies for distant-reading large collections of images. The chapter is dedicated to analytical techniques for studying (medium- or large-sized) image sets with a distant-reading approach (as opposed to close-reading smaller groups of images). The distant-reading approach can be used to identify recurring visual formats and themes within a collection of images, or to study the circulation and modification of images across online spaces.

Online images may also be studied in relation to their networked nature. Moving towards the network of images means moving outside the demarcated image that will now be studied alongside its digital context. That images are networked means they need to be considered 'not as solitary objects, but as a part of a network of other images, users, and platforms' (Niederer, 2018, p. 47). *Chapter 3* introduces methods for close-reading small sets of images, with a sensitivity towards their networked nature and the role of online platforms in ranking, formatting, and co-producing (visual) content.

The question of which images are deemed more visible than others online, thanks to the work of social media platforms and search engines in labelling and prioritizing content, is further explored in *chapter 4*. Here, we address the topic of inequalities in (visual) data sets, presenting techniques for studying bias in the visual representation of various issues online. We discuss successful images and present (visual) research methods aimed at understanding how and why specific images spread better than others.

Attending carefully to the missing (or unsuccessful) images in a folder is also at the centre of *chapter 5*, where we present participatory visual methods. Here, we turn the attention to what is missing from a collection of images and how to use participatory techniques to address this gap. Drawing from recent (data) feminist theories, which ask researchers to pay attention to societal power imbalances exacerbated by data-driven technology, we present visual strategies for participatory work. In this chapter, we ask which roles visual formats can play in designing participation in and with the digital, describing research settings and situations where participants are asked to *talk back* to the data.

Finally, we return to the entanglement of machines and humans in our visual culture, asking what kind of research one can do with machine-generated images. *Chapter 6* presents ways to do visual research with AI, using text-to-image models to explore machine biases and content moderation policies, or to co-design elicitation images for participatory practices that invite the collective imagination of social issues.

How to use this book

This book gathers a wide range of approaches for conducting research with and on digital images. It is also an attempt to shape and bring together in one place several years of research and experimentation on visual methods for digital research. The book is characterized by its diversity of methods, materials, and approaches. This means there are overlaps between the various techniques presented in different chapters, and the book is not exclusively organized around specific platforms or types of images. Indeed, the book deals with various image types, from social media images, search engine results, and AI-generated images to digital images explicitly captured in participatory workshops. Some chapters focus on a particular methodological approach, while others delve into the study of 'certain types' of images. For example, chapters 2 and 3 address specific methodo-logical approaches (i.e., distant and close reading of collections of images), while chapters 4 and 6 explore particular types of images.

In addition, a central theme in this book is the connection between the study of visual materials and the production of visual materials as a research tool: the different chapters explore both research on digital images and research using images. Despite the diversity of content, we have included links between chapters to create interactions between various methods, approaches, and materials. Readers could build their research project by mixing and matching the techniques presented in the chapters.

Depending on your needs, there are at least two main ways to use this book. If you are new to digital visual research and want to get an overview of available approaches and methods, the entire book will provide you with a (of course, incomplete) mapping of the field. Start with chapter 1, which introduces the specificity of digital images as a starting point for defining a methodological approach suited to studying them. If you already have a collection of images to study or display, each chapter also stands on its own to provide a different starting point for studying or using a collection of images. In case you do not yet have a collection of images, chapter 1 offers a comprehensive overview of techniques for creating one.

But, in the end, a book comes to life through its readers. If, by using this book, you find inspiration to incorporate existing, or even design new, methods for digital visual research, then the book will have achieved its purpose.

Acknowledgements

The visual, digital, and participatory research presented in this book is by no means a solitary endeavour. All of the projects we present here were undertaken with colleagues, students, or both. The Digital Methods Initiative at the University of Amsterdam is where we started collaborating during one of its early summer schools. Its rhythm of annual summer and winter schools, in which researchers from all over the world get together for week-long research projects, has offered a lively context for methodological innovation. Through its long-standing collaboration with Density Design at the Politecnico di Milano, it has incorporated a high standard in information design and data visualization as part of the research process. We thank the Digital Methods Initiative and Density Design for providing the opportunity and context to apply, develop, test, and improve many visual methods for digital research presented in this book. While the Digital Methods Initiative is definitely a place we consider part of our academic family, it is not our only research context.

Sabine developed her teaching and research interests at the Amsterdam University of Applied Sciences, from working as a cultural producer with Geert Lovink at the Institute of Network Cultures to eventually becoming a professor. Deep appreciation goes out to the Dean and close colleagues at the Faculty of Digital Media and Creative Industries, and the ARIAS platform for artistic research in Amsterdam, for their support and collaboration. Special thanks to the Visual Methodologies Collective, its past fellows and its current members – Janine Armin, Federica Bardelli, Carlo De Gaetano, Femke Dekker, Andy Dockett, Maarten Groen, Mariana Fernández Mora, Natalia Sánchez Querubín, Nienke Scholts, and Nick Verouden – and close collaborators Laura Cull, Patricia de Vries and Tamara Witschge, for cultivating an inspiring research environment of creativity, critical inquiry, and care.

For Gabriele, the Density Design research lab at the Department of Design in Politecnico di Milano has been the environment where a Ph.D. research project offered him the space to explore digital visual methods for the first time. Thanks to all the researchers and designers who contributed to this exceptional space throughout the years (Elena Aversa, Matteo Azzi, Andrea Benedetti, Agata Brilli, Ángeles Briones, Giorgio Caviglia, Daniele Ciminieri, Paolo Ciuccarelli, Tommaso Elli, Alessandra Facchin, Beatrice Gobbo, Michele Invernizzi, Michele Mauri, Azzurra Pini, and Giorgio Uboldi). Thank you to Donato Ricci, who (first in Milano and later in Paris) pushed towards studying digital images as a promising research line in the design field. And a special thanks to Federica Bardelli and Carlo De Gaetano for sharing an interest in breaking images and a fruitful academic and artistic collaboration dating back over ten years.

We would also like to thank Renato Bernasconi of *Diseña* for offering us the platform to further our collaboration around the study of images, which resulted in a special issue and many fruitful discussions about image research that laid the groundwork for this book.

The Public Data Lab, a collaborative context for digital researchers from various universities across Europe, illustrates the many international collaborations that have informed this book. We especially would like to thank Jonathan W. Y. Gray and Liliana Bounegru for exploring with us methods for visual analysis that inform some of the research presented in this book.

The various projects discussed in the chapters result from many collaborative efforts.

Chapter 1

In previous form, parts of this chapter have been published in G. Colombo, L. Bounegru, and J. Gray (2023). Visual models for social media image analysis: groupings, engagement, trends, and rankings. *International Journal of Communication*, 17(0), 28.

Chapter 2

Parts of this chapter have previously been published in S. Niederer (2018). *Networked Images: Visual Methodologies for the Digital Age*. Amsterdam University of Applied Sciences.

The study of #parisagreement presented in chapter 2 is part of a long-standing collaboration with Warren Pearce and Suay Ozkulay at Sheffield University, and Carlo De Gaetano of the Visual Methodologies Collective. Some of the methods for distant reading (such as the image colour maps and image clusters technique) were initially co-tested, refined, and documented for a module on Digital Methods for Internet Studies: Concepts, Devices and Data, convened by Liliana Bounegru and Jonathan W. Y. Gray at the Department of Digital Humanities, King's College London. The techniques for visual (participatory) analysis developed during the 'NATURPRADI' project (presented in chapters 2 and 5) are the results of collaboration with Donato Ricci, Agata Brilli, and Axel Meunier at Médialab – Sciences Po in Paris. The project studying a protest march on Twitter results from a collaboration with Matteo Azzi from the design studio Calibro. The study of visual imaginaries of the #amazonfires is part of a collaboration between Rina Tsubaki from the European Forest Institute and Jonathan W. Y. Gray and Liliana Bounegru at King's College London.

Chapter 3

The work on networked content analysis was developed by Sabine during a residency as a visiting scholar at the Annenberg School for Communication, University of Pennsylvania, a stimulating context for research on the representation of climate change in media content. Later, Klaus Krippendorff kindly wrote a preface to the *Networked Content Analysis* book, which was published with the Institute of Network Cultures.

The project about the circulation of junk content in high-engagement political spaces on Instagram during the 2019 Dutch provincial and European parliamentary elections was written up by Gabriele in collaboration with Carlo De Gaetano. The research was undertaken with Rama Adityadarma, Joris van Breugel, and Vic Krens during a data sprint organized by the Digital Methods Initiative at the University of Amsterdam.

In a follow-up data sprint, a collaboration of media researchers at the University of Amsterdam with colleagues in Belgium, Canada, Italy, the UK, and the US, and supported by First Draft, we developed the analysis of earnest, ambivalent, divisive, and non-divisive content. We would like to thank the participants in our project 'Problematic information and artificial amplification on Instagram in the run-up to the 2020 U.S. elections', Shemayra Bastiaanse and Jasemin Uysal. Thanks to Richard Rogers for including the research in the edited volume *The Propagation of Misinformation in Social Media*, published with Amsterdam University Press in 2023.

The study of climate visual vernaculars was conducted with Warren Pearce, Suay Ozkula, Natalia Sánchez-Querubín, and 2019 summer school participants: Jennifer Bansard, Philip Hutchison Barry, Andrea Benedetti, Sofie Burgos-Thorsen, Alessandra Cicali, Anne van den Dool, Laura Drakopulos, Beatrice Gobbo, Amanda Greene, Esther Hammelburg, Janna Joceli Omena, Phillip Morris, Alessandra Del Nero, Elaine Rabello, Rebekka Stoffel, Mischa Szpirt, Lauren Teeling, Emile den Tex, and Rasmus Tyge Haarloev.

The reflections on different types of composite images and the types of analysis they afford were formulated with Federica Bardelli as part of a joint contribution to 'We make the city' at Pakhuis de Zwijger, 2019.

Chapter 4

Parts of this chapter have been published in a previous form in L. Bogers, S. Niederer, F. Bardelli, and C. De Gaetano (2020). Confronting bias in the online representation of pregnancy.

Convergence: The International Journal of Research into New Media Technologies, 26(5–6), 1037–59: https://doi.org/10.1177/1354856520938606.

The study of the representation of (unwanted) pregnancy took place during a Digital Methods summer school of 2018 as part of the 'Retraining the machine' project, which Sabine co-facilitated with Loes Bogers and Carlo De Gaetano. Participants were: Sofía Beatriz Alamo, Carlo De Gaetano, Amber de Zeeuw, Nikolaj Frøsig, Mari Fujiwara, Pien Goutier, Lydia Kollyri, Nora Lauff, Frederike Lichtenstein, Felix Navarrete, Enedina Ortega Gutierrez, Claudia Pazzaglia, Sammy Shawky, Mischa Szpirt, Mandy Theel, Kim Visbeen, Anne Wijn, and Chuyun Zhang.

We also want to thank Giorgia Aiello and the participants of the 2016 Digital Methods winter school project 'A critical genealogy of the Getty Images Lean In Collection': Atossa Atabaki, Federica Bardelli, Erik Borra, Jorinde Bosma, Aliki Eleftheriadou, Alixia Garceau, Elias Gorter, Denise van Kollenburg, Katharina Lueke, Donato Ricci, Lotte van Rosmalen, Giovanna Salazar, Alexander Sommers, Charlot Verlouw, Anne Zwaan.

Chapter 5

The 'Urban belonging' project was a collaborative project of the Techno-Anthropology Lab at Aalborg University (DK), Service Design Lab – Aalborg University (DK), Gehl Architects (DK), Visual Methodologies Collective – Amsterdam University of Applied Sciences (NL), and the Center for Digital Welfare – IT University Copenhagen (DK). Its researchers were Sofie Burgos-Thorsen (DK), Drude Emilie Ehn (DK), Anders Koed Madsen (DK), Thorben Simonsen (DK), Sabine Niederer (NL), Maarten Groen (NL), Carlo De Gaetano (IT), Kathrine Norsk (DK), and Federico Di Fresco (AR). The 'Urban belonging' project is co-funded by the 'Doing Data Together' grant awarded to Anders Koed Madsen at Aalborg University and Innovation Fund Denmark's research grants awarded to Sofie Burgos-Thorsen and Drude Emilie Ehn, respectively. In addition, it is supported by Gehl, Service Design Lab (Aalborg University), Center for Digital Welfare (IT University Copenhagen), and Centre of Expertise for Creative Innovation in Amsterdam. Collaborators include Pedro Borges and community partners LGBTQ+ Denmark, Hugs &

Food, Danish Deaf Association, Danish Disability Association, SIND Denmark, and Mino Denmark. In 2023, the project was awarded the European Prize for Citizen Science Diversity & Collaboration Award.

Chapter 6

We owe a big thank you to Carlo De Gaetano for the collaboration, the discussions and joint experiments around generative visual AI, which prompted us to write a chapter on machine images.

The research for the project 'Prompting for biodiversity: visual research with generative AI', which we facilitated at the 2023 Digital Methods summer school in Amsterdam, was carried out in collaboration with Piyush Aggarwal, Bastian August, Meret Baumgartner, Tal Cohen, Sunny Dhillon, Alissa Drieduite, Xiaohua He, Julia Jasińska, Shaan Kanodia, Soumya Khedkar, Fangqing Lu, Helena Movchan, Janna Joceli Omena, Jasmin Shahbazi, Bethany Warner, Xiaoyue Yan, and co-facilitators Carlo De Gaetano and Maud Borie.

We also would like to thank the Communication Design master's students of the 2022/2023 Final Synthesis Design Studio at Politecnico di Milano (particularly Anna Cattaneo, Yiyuan Hu, Lara Macrini, Nicole Moreschi, Leonardo Puca, Silvia Sghirinzetti, Ce Zheng) for exploring the topic of bias in generative visual AI.

'After us the deluge' and the educational materials developed to engage adolescents and their parents in imagining a future with rising sea levels was a collaboration with various researchers from the Amsterdam University of Applied Sciences, including Janette Bessembinder, Adwin Bosschaart, Carlo De Gaetano, Marloes Geboers, Lisette Klok, Loes Kreemers, Sophie Postma, Reint Jan Renes, and Ingeborg Tiemessen, and the Royal Dutch Meteorological Institute (KNMI), and teachers and pupils from 4e Gymnasium secondary school in Amsterdam.

Many thanks to those who read and commented on early drafts of the chapter, including Erik Borra, Maarten Groen, Carlo De Gaetano and Natalia Sánchez Querubín.

1

Research with Images:
An Introduction

This chapter reviews theorizations and conceptualizations of digital images, such as the notion of networked images and the circulation and multiplication of images across online spaces. In the final section, it presents techniques for compiling collections of digital images.

Introduction

The sound of breathing. Inhale, exhale. A desktop with three files, titled GROSSE_FATIGUE_, HISTORY_OF_UNIVERSE and HISTORY_OF_UNIVERSE2. The cursor moves across a desktop image of the Milky Way, and the *Grosse Fatigue* video file comes to the fore. Another deep breath. Then, with the beat of a drum, two browser windows open.

A voice[1] starts speaking: 'In the beginning there was no earth, no water – nothing. There was a single hill called Nunne Chaha. In the beginning everything was dead. In the beginning there was nothing, nothing at all. No light, no life, no movement, no breath. In the beginning there was an immense unit of energy.'

As the poem unfolds, collections of images and videos rhythmically open and close, taking the viewer on an intense journey

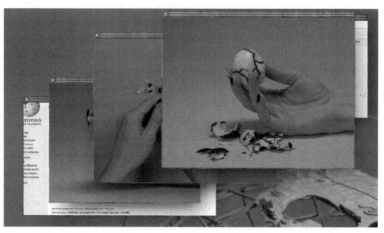

1.1 Still from *Grosse Fatigue* by Camille Henrot (2013).

through myths and sciences, making sense of the creation of the world (figure 1.1). The collections also form a commentary on collections, or the act of collecting, by capturing and observing 'other' cultures and other species.

Grosse Fatigue is clean and styled, in a mesmerizing mixture of hands leafing through art and history books and presenting objects against colourful backdrops, found online footage, videos of animals, and fragments filmed at the archives of the Smithsonian Institute. The windows through which the visual materials are presented open and close and are combined in various logics, by way of their shape, by way of their topic, by way of the poem that drives it forwards in a rhythmic narration of the beginning of the universe. By opening them together, side by side, overlaying, or in a meticulous stack ordered by size (figure 1.2), the images start a conversation with each other, with the backdrop, voice, and beat. The work can also be read as a creative response to the flattening power of search engines, which compile heterogeneous materials into apparently clean and homogeneous grids of content,[2] as the artist describes:

> Internet technology confronts us with an immensity of hetero-geneous and divergent material all reduced to the same level by the search engine. It's a flattening of the world, which is a violent experience for the mind. Our brains aren't prepared to absorb and

1.2 Still from *Grosse Fatigue* by Camille Henrot (2013).

cope with such a huge flow of information that it can't make sense of: this confrontation creates a sense of disarray. In this situation, it makes sense that the human mind would resort to the most efficient means of synthesizing information: myth and religion. (Henrot, 2017)

This 'flattening of the world' by search engines also resonates with theorizations of images as they circulate online. Immaterial, soft, poor, operational, invisible, ephemeral, and networked are just a few terms employed to characterize digital images. The digital turn in visual culture has given rise to a vast array of concepts that try to capture the specificity of online images, from their digital materiality to their multiplicity. This chapter introduces several theoretical and conceptual approaches to digital images. While discussing theories and concepts that scholars have used to describe various aspects of digital images, we also pay attention to the cultural products and artistic experiences that foreground their aesthetics.

When discussing aesthetics, we try to include not just what these images look like or how they may be perceived but also what they do – what Fuller and Weizman refer to as sensing and sense-making in their book *Investigative Aesthetics* (2021). For concepts concerning the online image, we do not aim to give an exhaustive overview, but rather stay close to the case studies presented throughout this book.

This chapter discusses theorizations and conceptualizations of digital images in four sections. Firstly, the digital image is examined in comparison to its analogue predecessor. This section characterizes digital images in terms of their digital materiality and the concerns arising from the disappearance of the difference between the original image and its copies.

Secondly, digital images are characterized as images that are meant for and processed by machines and need software to be rendered visible to the human eye. This section reviews some of the concepts that have been used to describe the new visual landscape where imaging practices are disconnected from human agency and vision. We review digital images' relationship with machine vision: the loss of images' representational power when they become part of data exchanges between machines, their intrinsic connection with the software, and their functioning without human agency, which renders them invisible to the human eye.

Thirdly, images are theorized as networked when they become part of socio-technical networks in which platforms and users co-shape their online visual content. Treating online images as networked content means that image research should not consider them as solitary objects but as part of a network of other related images, users, and platforms.

Lastly, networkedness leads to multiplicity. We explore the aesthetics and dynamics of image circulation, its adaptation, and commentary. With the dissolving distinction between the original and the copy and the need for software and hardware to render these immaterial images visible, it becomes apparent that digital images are seldom seen individually but always in multiple formations. Hashtags and other digital objects link one image to another, and their multiplicity is amplified as images are copied and moved across platforms and websites. As images move around and get hashtagged, commented on, or modified, their meaning constantly shifts through collaborative online practices. In this section, we introduce networkedness and circulation's effects on visual culture's dynamics and aesthetics.

The chapter explores each of these themes theoretically and through the critical analysis of art and design projects. Furthermore, the chapter reviews different strategies for compiling image collections, including sourcing from accounts, expert curation lists, keyword snowballing, and querying images to collect other images with computer vision. Finally, this chapter concludes by presenting the diverse approaches offered in this book to study collections of images with visual and digital methods.

Understanding digital images (in contrast to analogue)

Digital culture has led us to a wealth of new theories and concepts that address images in their digital state, often contrasted with analogue images. The most prominent theorization of the digital image builds on the work of Walter Benjamin and his influential work on art in the age of its mechanical reproducibility, and how the new photographic technologies would impact the place and status of the original artwork and its copies. When such concerns on the status of the image and its copies are brought to the digital realm, the question may involve the disappearance of the difference between the original and the copy. When the image is digital, does it matter whether we look at the original or an identical copy thereof? For instance, the conflation of the original image and its copy in the digital realm is captured by the notion of the 'Originalkopie' (Fehrmann et al., 2004). The digital copy may be spread widely in different sizes and quality levels, which will be discussed later in this chapter in the section on multiplicity.

Another recurring theme regarding the digitization of visual culture concerns the materiality of images. Images in the digital realm have been theorized as 'dematerialized' or 'immaterial' (Sassoon, 2004), having lost (or having never had) a material form. This new (im)materiality has resulted in the rise of different kinds of aesthetics, or visual styles, which attempt either to highlight or to obfuscate the digital composition of the image. From glitchy aesthetics to retro filters, an array of visual practices has emerged in dialogue with (or reacting to) the shift from analogue to digital in visual culture.

The glitch is a mode of image production in which the noise, flaws, interruption, and breakage of machines and their software press their mark on its output. 'The glitch is a wonderful experience of an interruption that shifts an object away from its ordinary form and discourse,' writes glitch artist and theorist Rosa Menkman in her *Glitch Studies Manifesto* (2009, p. 5). In her publication, she calls upon artists to become a 'nomad of noise artifacts!'. In her book *The Glitch Moment(um)* (Menkman, 2011), she also offers examples of what *glitch art* might look like, with digital artefacts produced by inserting errors in the underlying code of an image, which distorts the composition of the digital image (figure 1.3).

Where the glitch requires an attitude of experimentation and intricate work of bending and breaking, other digital image formats have been labelled 'lazy' (Nešović, 2022b). The screenshot, perhaps the laziest image of all, requires the screen capturing of an online image to reshare and recirculate. The 'lazy screenshot' has been observed as a contemporary digital practice that blurs the lines between human and machine involvement in creating and perceiving visual content (Nešović, 2022b). Similarly to the glitch, the screenshot, with its low resolution, deteriorated pixels, and cropped interface elements such as browser windows, is another format (or visual style) that speaks to the composition of the digital image. The screenshot has also been heralded as the 'banal sublime' (Nešović, 2022a), referring to this form of photographic document as the *main currency* of digital visual culture.

The screenshot is not just a digital-specific aesthetics, but it offers opportunities for studying visual online practices when, for example, it is used to recirculate particular contents across platforms and contexts. One example is a study of platform-specific visual styles in the depiction of climate change (as we

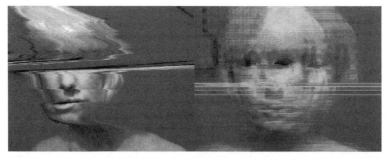

1.3 Rosa Menkman (2010). A Vernacular of File Formats, Glitched BMP (left) and Glitched Gif (right), *Selfportrait*.

discuss below), which found on Tumblr multiple screenshots depicting noteworthy exchanges from other social media sites, a practice researchers dubbed as 'environmental screenshotting' (Pearce et al., 2020). A similar outlook, in which different croppings and contexts of the lazy image are re-traced and collected with diligent research, is in a study concerned with the spread of misinformation on Twitter during forest fires. Here, following screenshotted content allowed researchers to identify a practice dubbed 'screenshot debunking', whereby screenshots of news articles and social media posts flagging misleading images of the fires have been shared widely during the event (Bounegru et al., 2022).

Where glitches, noise, and cropped screenshots foreground the digital composition of online images, retrograde and vintage-filtered images polish away their digital make-up, attempting to obfuscate the materiality of digital image production. Similarly to the wave of skeuomorphic interface design, representing digital items in the style of their real-world counterparts (e.g., the 'Save' icon as a floppy disk), the 'early rise of everyday social photography' has been characterized by 'an aesthetic saturated with nostalgia' (Jurgensen, 2019).

The style of digital images and 'social photos' (Jurgensen, 2019), triggered by the popularization of the smartphone app Hipstamatic and later on by Instagram with a larger set of (vintage) filters, has been described as nostalgic, making use of filters to add a warm, lo-fi, and analogue layer to the clean and cool aesthetics often associated with the digital. The early Instagram retro images (with faux-vintage filters, faded edges, and film grain) mimicking their printed counterparts disappeared slowly as digital photography became commonplace. However, Instagram (as well as other platforms, as we discuss below) can still be said to have its own (evolving) aesthetics (Leaver et al., 2020), which can be studied as 'style space' (Manovich, 2011c) with a focus on form and composition.

Images by and for machines

Another recurring theme in the theorization of digital images is their close connection with machines and the progressive removal of human agency in digital visual practices. Digital images are increasingly produced by and for machines in the first place, with human audiences often being out of the loop. Media scholars Ingrid Hölzl and Remi Marie (2015) speak of the 'soft image' (where 'soft' refers to software). The term 'soft image' captures a shift towards an image that is no longer produced with chemical processes but instead intrinsically merged with software in its production, fruition, and circulation.

The soft image loses its representational function and becomes a means of communication in non-human data infrastructures. In this view, images do not simply *represent* something (thus debates about their ability to faithfully capture the world fade to the background) but instead *do* something. Indeed, 'soft images' are machine-readable in that they are in a form that a computer can process or streamline to be scanned by machines, often before humans see them. While still looking similar to their analogue predecessor when displayed on a screen, soft images conceal various data processes primarily invisible to human eyes, from encoding format compressions to the complex algorithmic mechanisms of web platforms processing, analysing, and tagging images.

The loss of digital images' representational function was first noted by filmmaker and author Harun Farocki (2004), who coined the term 'operative image'. Operative (or operational) images do not represent, evoke, inform, or portray but instead are used by and for machines to perform a task. Farocki identified the military setting as a field where operative images could be observed, referring to the use of camera footage by unmanned aerial vehicles in the context of remote warfare. One could argue that similar processes have spread unprecedentedly and can be observed in a larger set of situations. Operative images are now embedded in autonomous cars; they are an essential part of medical imaging tools and geographic information systems; they are at the core of mapping and object recognition processes in industrial settings and constitute the backbone of surveillance infrastructures in our cities.

The notion of 'discorrelated images' (Denson, 2020) empha-sizes a disconnect between humans, digital images, and machines. In 'discorrelation', digital glitches, lens flares, and other similar visual artefacts are symbols and signals of 'a world of media not cut to human measure' (Denson, 2020, p. 3). Many authors have coined terms that capture this new visual landscape of 'non-human photography' (Zylinska, 2017), where imaging practices are disconnected from human agency and human vision. Today, most images online have probably been viewed by a machine but not necessarily seen by a human. Visual artist Trevor Paglen (2016) speaks of 'invisible images', referring to a visual culture where human vision is almost absent. With the term 'invisible', the focus is again on the absence of humans in today's digital visual culture and on the increasing importance of non-human algorithmic ways of seeing, such as computer vision systems constantly scanning the images we upload on social media platforms. If one were to look into one of these 'machine-to-machine seeing apparatuses', one would find a highly encoded flux of data, a 'menagerie of abstractions that seem completely alien to human perception' (Paglen, 2016, p. 16). Attempts have been made to put humans back in the loop, theorizing ways of 'seeing like a machine' (Ballvé, 2012) or designing ways to 'peek inside' these systems (Mordvintsev et al., 2015).

Exercises in unpacking the black box of computer vision, where researchers output so-called activation features (i.e., images that represent abstract features that the machine has learned to associate with specific concepts), are indeed aimed at 'letting us see through the eyes of the network' (Carter et al., 2019). Such endeavours to visualize machine vision processes have also resulted in a distinctive aesthetic, a psychedelic and surrealistic style, often referred to as '(deep) dreaming' after the first of these approaches popularized by Google (Mordvintsev et al., 2015). More recently, AI-generated images have been described as 'infographics about the dataset' (Salvaggio, 2022), referring to the possibility of using these images to study the training sets behind the machines used to generate them.

For researchers, the rise of massive machine vision infrastructures opens up new possibilities for seeing at scale. Computer vision, a term that captures the diverse range of algorithmic techniques for image analysis and classification, may be repurposed for analytical goals, such as clustering images by theme, identifying copies and variations, or quickly exploring the content of an image set. While having undisputed research potential, the computational analysis of large groups of images should be approached with care, also given current debates regarding the flaws and shortcomings of computer vision tools concerning issues of representation and discrimination (Buolamwini & Gebru,

2018; Crawford & Paglen, 2019; Sinders, 2020). The opaqueness of computer vision tools can also become a research object in itself, where one studies how images are parsed by web platforms' algorithms and reverse engineers the invisible processes of automated vision at play. Here lies another opportunity for image research, which focuses on studying biases in how algorithms analyse or rank images online. In what they call 'algorithm trouble', researchers (Meunier et al., 2021) studied the content posted on Twitter with hashtags #AIfail or #algorithmfail, and encountered examples of 'misclassification' ('Facebook thinks my channel is a restaurant'); misplaced recommendations ('The NRA is recommended to a depression and suicide awareness person?'); unrelated suggestions ('If we're out of plant-based cheese, would you like some plant-based flushable wipes?'); content moderation issues ('Rizzo, btw, is a horse'); humorous mis-targeting ('the internet does not get me at all', 'clearly they know me so well', 'thanks but no thanks'); problematic automated translations ('She is beautiful. He is clever. He understands math. She is kind'). A famous example of algorithmic flaws is the Twitter scandal, in which the cropping algorithm of the platform – which automatically crops an image to fit the preview in a tweet – demonstrated racial bias (Hern, 2020). The algorithmic exacerbation of existing injustice has given rise to feminist data practices, which will be further discussed in chapter 5.

Networked images

Many theories on the nature and agency of images in our society acknowledge a visual turn, also referred to as a 'pictorial turn' (Mitchell, 1992), recognizing an increasing centrality of visual materials in our society. However, many of the current concepts surrounding online images and digital visual culture focus on theorizing the single image without considering its networked status. Online images become 'networked' when users like, share, comment, or tag them and when platforms and engines format, filter, feed, and recommend them to others. Images may also be networked across platforms through their circulation when the same image is fed to or otherwise resonates on different platforms and websites (as is the case with memetic content discussed in the next section). That images are networked means they need to be considered not as solitary objects but as a part of a network of other images, users, and platforms. To complicate matters, people and platforms do not all network images (and other content) in the same way. Platforms have distinct ways of networking, ranking, and presenting visual and textual content (figure 1.4). Therefore, digital image research has to consider the different ways of demarcating content beyond the single image and consider the entire network of related content, actors, platforms, and websites surrounding online images (Niederer, 2019).

The networked character of online images suggests a methodological shift that does not consider the textual and numerical as an addition to the visual but as an inherent part of the social media image itself. Hashtags, timestamps, comments, and metadata link one image to another, generating networks of associated items. Such contextual elements (tags, texts, comments, timestamps) can be used to make sense of and interpret what images do online. Researchers have noted that studying digital images cannot leave aside these non-visual elements. Images' content should inform the analysis 'just as much as tags and words surrounding images do' (Geboers & Van de Wiele, 2020, p. 753). In this regard, there have been calls to shift from the term 'image' to more inclusive terms. For example, to address the entanglement of visual, textual, and numerical elements at play on a page online, the notion of 'photographic document' (Neal, 2010) considers the image as only one part of a larger ecosystem of digital objects on offer for research.

Taking into serious consideration the work platforms do in co-producing content opens up new possibilities for image research. This technicity, or the specific ways in which platforms and engines serve, format, redistribute, and essentially co-produce content, becomes an essential point of consideration in the study of digital visual culture when 'tracing associations' (Latour, 2005) between images and their carriers and their online publics (or: users). Taking networkedness and technicity of content as a methodological entry point, it becomes clear that images should not be studied as separate from their network but rather *as a group*. Much of the image analysis work done today starts with a folder of images (Colombo, 2019), along with information and metadata about their location, user engagement, and other variables. This point of departure means that ongoing research

TWITTER

Sustainable Energy @Sustainablehero 30 giu
Major #heatwave over North America, @realDonaldTrump want to talk
#ClimateChange #GlobalWarming now or will you wait till January again? We
will #ActOnClimate without you! You can't stop the rise of Clean technology
worldwide! A message from your friendly neighborhood #Superhero

Traduci il Tweet

3   5

Users   Hashtags   @Mentions   Images   Reactions

INSTAGRAM

everydayclimatechange • Follow
Edinburgh, United Kingdom

everydayclimatechange "There is no
alternative planet." – photo by @jshphotog –
One of many placards at the weekend's
#antiTrump rally held in #Edinburgh,
#Scotland. #everydayclimatechange
#climatechange #climate #environment
#resist #resistoften #JeremySuttonHibbert
mariehelene #alternatibatour
#alternatiba #alternatibalimousin

safetyfluff Paris climate accord did nothing
to fix the environment. And put all the
burden on america

jaaared_ By the time the planet is in peril we
will be dead

rjshawkins The as above this post for
Amazon Prime day,,, Says it all really

subliminalmessenger @jaaared_ is that a
good reason to not try to improve?

Users   Hashtags   @Mentions   Images   **2,440 likes**
Reactions   Comments   Locations   JULY 16

Add a comment   ...

1.4 Modified screenshots of Twitter and Instagram posts, annotated to highlight
the opportunities the interface presents to users to network their content. Each
platform and engine handles images differently, thereby revealing platform-
specific technicities. The networkedness and technicity of online images call for
an approach attuned to the medium.

questions cannot be answered by studying only a single image stripped of its context. One example is the study of how images circulate, are engaged with, appropriated, made into memes, and changed over time. The networkedness of images calls for new conceptualizations and visual methodologies that can adapt to this networkedness.

The distinct ways platforms have of networking, ranking, and presenting content, as well as the specific actions they grant to users, promote platform-specific cultures of use, resulting in platform vernaculars: a combination of 'styles, grammars, and logics' (Gibbs et al., 2015, p. 257) native to (or characteristic of) a particular platform. Platforms' features stimulate particular communicative patterns, or platform vernaculars, which result in the production of platform-specific content, such as 'rants on blogs, tweet storms on Twitter' or 'long-forms on Medium' (Rogers, 2017b, p. 1). Applied to image research, this entails that different platforms have their own visual language that can be compared when, for instance, looking at the representation of a single issue across platforms (see chapter 3). Platform vernaculars may also refer to specific stylistic elements, as discussed by media scholar Lev Manovich for Instagram and its specific *mise-en-scène*, which he describes as a 'construction of scenes and images that are atmospheric, visually perfect, emotional without being aggressive, and subtle as opposed to dramatic' (2017b, p. 81). Indeed, attending to the work that platforms do in co-producing content opens up possibilities for cross-platform analysis, where one compares 'visual vernaculars' (Niederer, 2018; Pearce et al., 2020) across platforms concerning a particular issue. On the other side, one could follow 'generic images' (Anderson et al., n.d.) as they are used across different sites and platforms, paying attention to how circulation contributes to adding new meanings to the same image when used in different contexts.

The diffusion of networked images also opens up a way to study affective publics that are assembled through shared sentiment, opinion, or affect (Papacharissi, 2014; Geboers, 2022). Studying the ways in which such publics repurpose existing images (e.g., by turning them into memes or creatively appropriating them by using filters and other visual and textual elements) provides new insights into the dynamic user cultures of a particular platform or even traversing platforms.

The multiplicity of digital images

As we have pointed out, online images are rarely experienced individually but more often in groups, threads, sets, grids (Lister, 2013, p. 8), or even in 'filmic' formats such as the stream (Sze, 2018). Hashtags, timestamps, and other metadata link one image to another, generating networks of connected items, making multiplicity an important feature of online images. Artists and designers have worked with digital-found materials to expose such multiplicity. As a case in point, artist Penelope Umbrico has collected sunset pictures from the photo-sharing platform Flickr, presenting them in an ever-growing grid. The artwork's title is updated constantly with the number of results one gets from searching the word [sunset] on the platform. In 2016, the title read: *30,240,577 Suns (from Sunsets) from Flickr*. For another iteration of the work, titled *Sunset Portraits (2010–ongoing)*, Umbrico filtered the same set of Flickr sunset images to retain only the portraits in which the 'technology of the camera is exposing for the sun, not the people in front of it, thereby erasing the subjectivity of the individual' (Umbrico, 2010). The larger set was curated to show grids with the (still enormous) collection of dark silhouettes against bright-coloured sunsets. Figure 1.5 shows the grid in 2013 containing 1,539 images out of the 13,243,857 sunset photos.

Compiling collections of similar content, as is the case with the grid of sunsets from Penelope Umbrico, is just one of many examples of cultural production that directly engages with the intrinsic multiplicity of digital images. Multiplicity here refers not only to abundance (in that there are arguably *more* images produced daily) but more specifically to the grouping formats through which images are viewed in various online spaces. Such multiplicity has been paired with (or has given rise to) a set of artistic practices and vernacular cultural production that deals with a particular aesthetic of compiling and composing. The term 'assembly' refers to a cultural form that 'places expressive relationships front and center' (Parry, 2023, p. 3). From the ironic juxtaposition of competing concepts in memes and image macros to the resurgence of catalogues as a communicative format, 'assembly' as a cultural form can be defined as 'any combination of expressive elements that maintains and seizes on

1.5 Penelope Umbrico (2013), *Sunset Portraits from 13,243,857 Sunset Pictures on Flickr on 10/08/13*. Installation comprised of 1,539 machine c-prints, on display at the Orange County Museum of Art, CA.

the appearance of selection and arrangement' (Parry, 2023, p. 3). On Instagram, one can find a myriad of catalogue curators who repurpose the grid of their personal accounts to create the most disparate collections of images (including fruit stickers, Japanese glass textures, and train seat fabrics). In one telling instance of these Instagram catalogues, the grids are of recurrent visual tropes on the platform (e.g., a person on a lake dock shot from behind, a close-up of a hand reaching to a beautiful landscape in the background, a hand holding a maple leaf against yet another bucolic scene). The account, named 'Insta Repeat', archives and exposes image repetitions on the platform, becoming an echo chamber of Instagram's visual tropes.

The aesthetics of compiling and assembling not only is embraced by artists and cultural creators who curate collections of images displayed in art galleries and Instagram profiles, but can be found at the centre of various vernacular digital practices. Many are instances in which different actors generate content through the juxtaposition of elements, exploring the power of assembly 'to move audiences and mobilise publics, and just as crucially, to do harm' (Parry, 2023, p. 2). One example is the evidence collage, defined in the Media Manipulation Casebook

(2020) as 'a collection of screenshots and text assembled into a shareable document and presented as evidence'. Evidence collages, often pasting images and screenshots from various sources with graphic elements, are usually produced with basic image editing applications and employed to disseminate often unverified information.[3]

The multiplicity of digital images is also amplified by their circulation, as images are copied and moved around across platforms and websites. With the term 'circulationism', artist and theorist Hito Steyerl refers to a new visual online regime where the circulation of images outshines their production (Steyerl, 2013). The primacy of circulation can also be noted in the shift from online 'repositories of images', such as Flickr, based on archiving and classification, to 'infrastructures of circulation' (smartphones and social media platforms), which promote effortless sharing and fast circulation (Hand, 2020, p. 312). In the project 'Reblogs or context is the new content', designer-researcher Silvio Lorusso (2015) visualizes 'the trail created by a single digital image while travelling through a social platform' (figure 1.6). The project presents a video montage of the same image, 'reblogged' – to use the term of the platform – by Tumblr

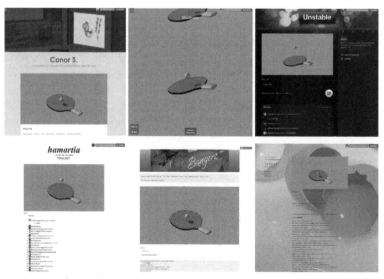

1.6 Images from the 'Reblogs or context is the new content' project, by designer-researcher Silvio Lorusso (2015).

users on their personal pages. The project illustrates the multiplicity of digital images circulating in different online spaces.

Some commentators see this 'circulationism' (Steyerl, 2013) as a signal of the unstable nature of the digital image, as its meaning is constantly shifting through collaborative online practices. The circulation of digital images online accelerates a hectic process of constant modification. While travelling around, images get remixed, downsized, previewed, thumbnailed, or otherwise modified, rendering them 'ephemeral' (Hand, 2017), 'fugitive and transient' (Lister, 2013). Such instability requires image researchers to develop adaptive methods attuned to the instability and multiplicity of images in flux (Niederer & Colombo, 2019).

In the publication 'in defense of the poor image', the artist and theorist Hito Steyerl celebrates the phenomenon of the 'copy in motion' (2009). The fact that images may be circulated, remixed, and reappropriated and may have an afterlife is one of the strong points of digital visual culture rather than a threat. Through the visualization of groups of (circulated) images, or 'metapicturing', such poor images can be reunited with their original (Rogers, 2021) and studied as collections. Others coined the term 'thumbnail visibility', noting how fleeting and casual ways of seeing images in groups, often at reduced size, ask for an increasing 'simplicity of style, content and form' (Frosh, 2013, p. 144). Referring to memetic production, Shifman (2014) notes how image manipulation may result in upscaled versions as users 'repackage' content through mimicry and remixing, generating collections of related and similar content. The notion of the internet meme as a 'group of digital items' with shared features and created with 'awareness of each other' (Shifman, 2014) instead of a 'cultural unit that propagates' (as the term was first used) invites researchers to approach online images in groups.

Compiling collections of images

The features of digital images discussed above point towards the collection of images as a research object. The shift 'from image to network' (Lister, 2013), the rise of infrastructures of circulation, and the multiple ways in which images duplicate online make the singularity of digital images fade into the background. It becomes clear that images should not be studied as solitary objects separated from their network but in groups. In a visual research setting that takes networkedness and technicity of content as a methodological entry point, much of the analytical work often starts with the compilation of a folder of images and their metadata.

The argument in favour of studying images in groups does not stand in opposition to those interpretive traditions that value close engagement with images. The folder of images approach does not mean that researchers need to abandon (or reject altogether) interpretive approaches that take a 'very attentive stance' (Rose, 2016, p. 10) towards images, even if, given the unprecedented amount of visual material available online, questions of sustainability of this kind of approach arise. Instead, this point of departure means that ongoing research questions cannot be answered by studying only a single image stripped from its context. For example, one may need to study how images are appropriated, made into memes, and changed over time while they circulate, or study the varying levels of engagement that different copies of the same image may receive in various online spaces. These research questions do not necessarily discard the close reading of individual images as an interpretive strategy. However, they require the identification of collections of content (i.e., folders of images) as a methodological entry point.

How to assemble groups of digital images? Now that we have established how online images may be networked, otherwise related, circulated, and better approached as a collection of items, this section explores means to compile such collections. In the following chapters, we will distinguish between approaches for studying large image sets (chapter 2) and for smaller sets (chapter 3). But, first, we briefly introduce five strategies for compiling folders of images: source-based, expert-curated, query-based, and its related approach of snowballing keywords, and image-based collection-building. Each of these strategies is described, addressing the starting points for the collection (such as a list of terms or sources) and the means of collecting images. We also offer a scenario for each strategy to illustrate the types of questions and analyses one could do with each data collection technique.[4] These strategies (and others) will be detailed in the case studies and sample projects presented in the following chapters.

Source- or account-based collections

This first strategy starts from a set of sources, be they websites or user accounts, that are relevant to the issue under study. This list of sources can follow from a stakeholder analysis or a news analysis. One can also start from expert lists (e.g., taken from a Wikipedia page, conference website, or other online inventory). Another option is to create a list from a search engine query aimed at collecting authoritative sources related to a specific issue (according to a search engine ranking algorithm). This groundwork is necessary to establish the 'authorities' or the leading organizations in the field, or who are the most relevant spokespeople for a particular issue. The next step is collecting user accounts or website URLs and compiling image sets (and metadata) from their posts or websites.

Account-based collections of images, particularly those starting with a list of authoritative sources, are useful when taking official or policy accounts as a baseline for studying a social issue across social media websites. For example, one can start by analysing an IPCC (Intergovernmental Panel on Climate Change) account and how it covers and depicts climate change, then compare the official representation with the most-engaged posts across platforms. Here, the IPCC account coverage (perhaps combined with other official sources) can function as a baseline, offering the official experts' voice to be compared with how it contrasts or resonates with what is posted and engaged with on social media.

Expert-curated collections

This second strategy is closely related to the first and entails collaborating with experts and asking them what the essential sources and materials to collect and study are. When an in-person exchange (online/offline) is impossible, one could start from the experts' accounts and collect the sources mentioned in their posts. This way, you indirectly use source collection (the first strategy) to compile an expert-curated collection (the second strategy).

A scenario of use can be to invite experts on microplastics to share relevant sources, materials, and keywords on the topic, to compile a collection of sources for a study on the perceived human health risks of microplastics as they resonate in online news coverage.

Query-based collections

A third strategy consists of querying search engines and social media platforms to collect sets of images. Starting from the aforementioned expert-based approach, researchers can compile lists of expert terms and keywords when discussing a particular topic. Such terms can be compiled together or derived from an expert interview, in which the expert is invited to discuss the matter as if the interviewer is a fellow expert (and the researcher notes keywords, retaining the jargon and specialist vocabulary). When an in-person (online/offline) exchange is not possible, an expert keyword list can also be derived from online materials, such as interviews with experts, their publications, or (video) lectures. Regardless of how keyword lists are compiled, the work involves understanding 'who is using them, in which contexts, and with what spread or distribution over time' (Rogers, 2017, p. 81). Once compiled, keywords are queried on a search engine or social media platform to collect relevant images (or posts) which are subsequently studied.

When an issue is contested or controversial, researchers may be interested in querying its programme (the official account) and its anti-programme (its critique and counternarratives) to explore who and what resonate in each of these spaces. The 'programme' and 'anti-programme' approach entails identifying competing terms (and possibly also those that are an attempt at neutrality) and comparing the results. For example, querying for 'gun ownership' (as the programme keyword) and 'gun control' (as the anti-programme keyword) can be an entry point to studying different sides of the debate about guns and tracing its alliances, sources, spokespeople, stakeholders, and visual language. In a study of Instagram images, 'gun ownership' and 'gun control' are used to collect the most-engaged images in the run-up to US elections. The two image collections are compared to assess the divisiveness of the two competing spaces (see chapter 3). Another example of programme and anti-programme visual research is a study comparing Instagram images for #lovewins and #jesuswins after the United States Supreme Court ruling on same-sex marriage (Baccarne et al., 2015). The two sets are used to identify memetic practices that become part of the debate (such as overlaying images with a rainbow filter in one space and a white cross on a red background in the opposite space).

Collections with keyword (or hashtag) snowballing

A fourth strategy is to use the metadata of an initial collection to grow the data set through snowballing techniques. With snowballing, one starts from a known list of keywords (or hashtags) and expands the list by tracing their associations online. A co-hashtag network is a fairly straightforward way of doing this, where one takes hashtags from social media posts (using, for instance, Instagram, TikTok, or Twitter data as a starting point) and maps the co-hashtags that occur in combination with those in the initial data set. Relevant hashtags found through this analysis can then be added to the keyword list used for data collection.

One example is a study of eco-fiction genres on Instagram, where researchers used a co-hashtag analysis to retrieve hashtags that were used in combination with the climate fiction hashtag #cli-fi (De Gaetano et al., 2022). They then selected the most frequently recurring ones related to eco-fiction and expanded the keywords list. In order to find content related to the various eco-genres on Instagram and to delve further into the variety of hashtags used by those communities to define their aesthetic, hone it, or connect to other ones, the expanded hashtag list was then used as a starting point for a new query.

Image-based querying

An entirely different strategy from the textual ones described so far is the visual approach that takes an image as a starting point. The image set, in this case, is based on a particular image whose copies and instances are reunited through data collection. Starting from one (or more) specific images, one can use services for reverse image search that, by means of computer vision algorithms, match similar images and return web pages that host them. It is a technique for compiling collections of images that enable circulation research. Using tools such as Google Web Search's 'reverse image search' enables researchers to see how specific images are put to use in different online contexts (Aiello & Parry, 2020; Rogers, 2021) and to study the resonance and circulation of particular imagery.

With image-based querying, choosing the starting image(s) is crucial. It could be a particularly controversial image, but the technique also works with a (curated) collection as a starting point. One example is a project that investigates the use of the Getty Images Lean In photo collection. This stock photo collection was hailed as groundbreaking because it depicted women in powerful positions (rather than in a sexualized or maternalized fashion). Researchers queried the Lean In Collection on Google Image reverse search to analyse how images were circulated online, in order to find how their usage reiterated bias (Aiello & Parry, 2020).

Conclusion

In a digital visual research setting, one often begins with a folder of images containing images compiled with one of the strategies described above (or a combination of these). To use a term from design research, the scenario of use is a folder full of images and their metadata, open to interpretation. The folder of images is not just a metaphor that captures the analytical shift towards the collection of images but also represents a very practical situation. After research questions are formulated, a list of sources is compiled, and visual content is located and collected, researchers often find themselves with a collection of images (saved in a local or shared folder or as a list of available image URLs). At this point, the need to look into the collection arises. In the following chapters, we illustrate and discuss various strategies to approach various kinds of (online) image collections and the kind of research questions one can answer with them.

In the next chapter, we detail various displaying formats for collections of images, and we present strategies for distant-reading large image collections. Chapter 2 is dedicated to analytical techniques for studying (medium- or large-sized) image sets with a distant-reading approach (as opposed to close-reading smaller groups of images). The distant-reading approach can be used to identify recurring visual formats and themes within a collection of images, or to study the circulation and modification of images across online spaces.

Further Readings

- Aiello, G., & Parry, K. (2020). *Visual Communication: Understanding Images in Media Culture*. London: SAGE Publications.
- Rogers, R. (2019). *Doing Digital Methods*. Thousand Oaks, CA: SAGE Publications.
- Steyerl, H. (2009). In Defense of the Poor Image. Retrieved from e-flux website: www.e-flux.com/journal/10/61362/in-defense-of-the-poor-image.

2

Distant Images: Reading Large Collections

This chapter introduces techniques for distant reading large collections of digital images while considering their limitations and advantages. It demonstrates techniques for grouping images by formal similarity, content, and digital features such as hashtags and chronology. The chapter ends with a consideration of the ethical implications of displaying online images in research outputs and the role of visualizations as analytical tools for large image collections.

Introduction

A boy lies down in a valley made of photographs, smiling as he looks at a picture he has picked up off the ground. For an installation by Erik Kessels displayed in 2012 at the FOAM museum in Amsterdam, the artist printed every picture posted to the photo-sharing website Flickr.com on a single day. As a result, the museum's rooms are flooded with piles of images, where visitors can experience the feeling of swimming – or drowning – in a sea of visual content, and be surprised by the tremendous amount shared within only 24 hours on just one platform (figure 2.1). The growing number of images shared online may similarly overwhelm researchers interested in studying the visual. The availability of visual material raises new methodological challenges of 'scope, scale, and selection' (Hand, 2017, p. 216): if images are everywhere, where do we look? The data selection phase becomes crucial, both conceptually and practically. At the same time, the wealth of visual content available online may trigger a data-greedy attitude, where researchers put an excessively optimistic emphasis on the size of the image collection or, as noted in early criticisms of Big Data research, adhere to the 'problematic underlying ethos that ... quantity necessarily means quality' (boyd & Crawford, 2011, p. 6).

Facing an oversaturated visual era, coupled with the profusion of computational tools for large-scale data analysis, the temptation is indeed that of fetishizing size and ignoring context, a research outlook that data-feminism scholars have referred to as 'totalizing fantasies of world domination as enacted through data capture and analysis' (D'Ignazio & Klein, 2020b, p. 151). In this chapter, we embrace these criticisms and offer ways into large collections of images that acknowledge the limitations of large-scale automated image analysis. While

2.1 A photo of the artwork *24 Hrs in Photos*, by Erik Kessels, as presented at FOAM Amsterdam in 2012.

approaching images in groups, we still value the close reading of individual images.

Where the example of the piles of images speaks to the imagination, when studying large collections of images, the research process often entails the arrangement of images in a particular configuration. In other words, images are 'analytically displayed' (Rogers, 2021) to support interpretive work. In this context, data visualization, and in particular forms of direct visualization (Manovich, 2011b) that retain images in the output, becomes a crucial step in the analysis, not just as the aesthetic culmination of the analysis (Niederer & Colombo, 2019) or as a sort of materialization of the media reveals (Allen, 2020) that represent the endpoint of most digital research. Data visualization is instead considered a functional tool in a more elaborate analytical procedure to support and actively co-produce the analysis. The choice of which arrangement of images to design is crucial and, as said above, constitutes an integral part of the analytical process. Similarly to what has been said concerning software development in digital research, the choices in displaying images in visual research have 'epistemological repercussions' (Borra & Rieder, 2014) and thus must be approached critically. The question is how different image arrangements may promote various interpretive procedures and which arrangement is suitable for a particular analysis (and not for others), always keeping in mind that visual models are not innocent but embed specific forms of knowledge (Drucker, 2014). The output of this process can be described as a 'composite image' (Colombo, 2018), as one makes a new image combining multiple ones in the same optical space. The analytical display of image sets can also be referred to as 'metapicturing' (Rogers, 2021), as it produces an image that is used to reflect on other images (Mitchell, 1994; Grønstad & Vågnes, 2006).

This chapter is dedicated to research techniques for studying (medium- or large-sized) image sets with a distant-reading approach (as opposed to close-reading smaller groups of images). The term 'distant' here refers to the point of view of the researcher, who zooms out from the material and adopts a bird's-eye view to discern and appreciate patterns that would otherwise go unnoticed. Often performed with the help of software, with distant reading one studies the recurrence of particular formal features (e.g., the use of colours or textures) or the dominance of formats and content types in a collection (e.g., memes, screen-shots, or illustrations).

Another application of distant reading is image circulation research, where one traces the reappearance of the same image (or a copy thereof) within a set. Although the approach benefits from zooming out as a key analytical move, the bird's-eye view is not considered the endpoint but rather an intermediate research-process step, in which one retains the full collection of images to facilitate moving from the aggregated view to the individual images. Large-scale software-assisted visual analysis often falls short in capturing digital images' layered and expressive meanings (Rose, 2016). In response to such critiques, distant reading here should not be considered the endpoint of the research process but rather instrumental to the selection (Geboers, 2022) of individual images in the set (e.g., recurrent, dominant, similar ones), which are subsequently analysed individually. The distant view is thus a tool that supports close engagement with specific images in the set (and not others).

There are key aspects to the distant-reading approach. First, as mentioned above, the research process builds on a particular way of looking at image sets: from a distance. Zooming out is an analytical move (albeit not the final one) that enables the obser-vation of visual patterns. Second, the techniques presented here have the collection of images as their primary research object (manually compiled or with tool-assisted processes): images are approached not only from afar but also en groupe. Looking at images together departs from the realization that most digital visual practices, from image circulation to memetic cultures, are inherently multiple and involve many images at once. The approach to digital images en groupe benefits from the design of custom displaying formats: images are arranged in a particular configuration that supports their analytical interpretation.

These features – zooming out and displaying formats – are briefly taken in turn by looking at research practices (including those in arts and design) that employ them. The chapter follows with a demonstration of the distant-reading approach, presenting an array of different techniques for studying large collections of images. The analytical approaches presented in this chapter are well suited for answering a wide range of research questions. For example, the distant-reading approach can be used to detect recurring visual formats and themes in a collection of images, and possibly to analyse these visual patterns over time. In addition, distant reading of large collections of images can help to study the circulation and modification of images across online spaces (including those that are copied, modified, or result from memetic practices). Moreover, when images are displayed alongside other digital objects (e.g., hashtags and reactions), the distant-reading approach can also help to study how images are reacted to online. Alongside different research techniques, the chapter also offers an overview of display formats that can be used to perform various analyses, including image colour maps (where images are clustered based on formal similarity), image clusters (with images grouped by content with computer vision), image timelines and image networks (where images are clustered based on shared digital features such as hashtags or timestamps).

Zooming out: distance as a vantage point

With distant reading, one starts by zooming out from an image set. Zooming out, or looking at a distance, is quite a decisive analytical move that allows researchers to observe patterns of repetitions and appreciate resonances and similarities among the images in a collection. Distance as a vantage point can be traced back to various research traditions. More recently, distance as a method has been pioneered in literary studies by Franco Moretti, to whom the popularization of the phrase 'distant reading' is owed. The term is used to characterize an approach to literary criticism that sees distance as a form of knowledge rather than an obstacle (Moretti, 2013). Often applied to an author's complete *oeuvre* or a whole corpus of an entire genre, distant reading (computer-assisted) usually outputs graphical renditions (networks or diagrams) that expose correlations among elements or stylistic patterns.

With the term 'Cultural Analytics', Lev Manovich (2020) put forward a programme for the computational analysis of cultural data sets. Aptly summarized with the question of 'How to See One Billion Images?', the research effort is that of analysing cultural production at scale to observe patterns and trends. Cultural Analytics outputs are software-assisted arrangements of large image sets, displayed according to formal features such as colour hue or lightness. Probably the most popular format is the so-called *photoplot* (Manovich, 2012), constructed as a traditional scatter plot visualization that retains images (instead of translating them into graphical marks). It is used to study coarse visual shifts in a corpus, such as the portrait waning in favour of the composition on the covers of a magazine (Manovich, 2010) or moments of abrupt change in a painter's *oeuvre* (Manovich, 2011a). First applied to digitized artefacts (paintings, magazine covers, comic books), the approach has subsequently expanded to analyse social media content, with large sets of images displayed chronologically to follow an event unfolding over time. In one example, photos from the Brooklyn area during Hurricane Sandy, sorted by time of upload and hue, reveal the 'visual rhythm' of the event (Hochman et al., 2013) through the recurrent shifts of dark and light colours (indicating day and night), and the abrupt darkening of colours (corresponding to power outage).

In the Cultural Analytics approach, the argument is that, given the unprecedented amount of cultural artefacts produced today, one needs new (computational) methods to look at them at scale (Manovich, 2020). Zooming out is framed as an opportunity connected to technological possibilities and a response to an unprecedented abundance of visual material; zooming out to see more and differently because abundance requires it and because it is possible. Here we embrace this approach, but, at the same time, we still value the close reading of images. Distance is an intermediate step in the research process, constantly moving from the distant to the close view.

The Cultural Analytics approach to studying large image corpora is often referred to as 'visualisation without reduction' (Manovich, 2011b), as the outputs retain images (instead of translating them into graphical marks). In this chapter, we explore ways of zooming out from a set of images, aware of how this constitutes a form of visual reduction. But it is precisely thanks to this reduction that distant reading offers an unexpected way into collections of visual materials, allowing for the detection of novel patterns from a distance.

Looking at images together: display formats

In the distant-reading approach, one considers images *together*. Images are treated as a collection of content (either compiled manually or with the help of tools) and looked at *en groupe*. The analytical techniques benefit from arranging images in the same optical space. The move recalls the literary format of the list, which gives 'unity to a set of objects no matter how dissimilar among themselves' (Eco, 2009). When displayed together, images comply with 'contextual pressure' (Eco, 2009) and are interpreted as a group for being found in the same place.

When it comes to the digital realm, there is quite a strong rationale for looking at images together. The image collection as a research object follows and repurposes the grouping formats in which images are experienced and organized online (Colombo, 2018). As images on the web are increasingly seen in multiple formations (e.g., the grid, the list, the slideshow, the stream), looking at image sets enables studying visual practices specific to digital culture. For example, one can trace patterns of circulation (following which images travel online and how) or observe dynamics of repetition and modification (studying, say, how images are visually altered, turned into memes, or otherwise modified).

From the pervasive use of mood boards in various design traditions to contact sheets, once a staple of the photographer, the image collection has its history as a tool for visual research. One can trace it back to the architectural fantasies of the eighteenth-century Venetian painting style capriccio, a form of eye-teasing achieved by compositing impossible images. More recently, artists and photographers have creatively exploited the format for visual research. A case in point is the work of German artists Hilla and Bernd Becher. In their *Typologies of Industrial Buildings* (2004), the collection (or catalogue) is a tool to appreciate differences and similarities among a set of images. Such typologies display (side by side in a grid-like format) photos of industrial structures with similar functions to invite viewers to compare shapes, forms, and designs across regional differences and periods.

Similarly, Dutch photographers Ari Versluis and profiler Ellie Uyttenbroek (2002) compiled portraits of individuals to expose stereotypes in self-presentation. Each portrait photo, with subjects standing in identical poses, further emphasizing their conformity to a particular dress code, is presented in a 12-square grid dedicated to a specific social group and its associated style or subcultural identity. Portraits are collected in thematic catalogues with telling titles such as Casual Queers, Gabbers, Techno Hippies, Farmcore, Surfistas, and French Touch. The project, named 'Exactitudes', exploits the visual format of the image grid as a tool for visual research. Individually, each portrait is pretty unremarkable, but when they are aggregated in a grid and looked at 'together' in the same space, each becomes part of a meaningful collection that captures a particular zeitgeist.

The visual format of the image collection is also at the core of notable place-based investigations across photography and visual ethnography. One example is Ed Ruscha's project on the Los Angeles sunset strip, dubbed *Every Building on the Sunset Strip* (1966), a 25-foot accordion-folded book with two continuous photographic views of the street, one for each side of it. The book, a sort of pre-digital Google Street View, offers a seamless view of an urban landmark in a compact form, recomposing its photographic fragments.

Similarly, in the work of digital artist Jenny Odell, aggregation and collection are a means for foregrounding details in large visual corpora, which would otherwise go unnoticed. In one of the artworks, dubbed 'peripheral landscapes', she collects decorative elements from the margins of old digitised maps and creates three tableaux collecting images of People, Gods, and Flora/Fauna. The apparently only ornamental components, brought to the foreground thanks to their collection, are indeed 'more telling of the times than the cartographers could have ever known' as they 'preserve traces of colonialism, heliocentrism, superstition and more' (Odell, 2015). The aggregation in the same space brings to the foreground peripheral elements found at the margins of different maps, giving them a unity that puts them in dialogue with each other. Regardless of the medium and type of material, these experiences deploy the collection as a format for visual research. Images are collected in the same optical space to look at them in conversation with each other and bring forward their shared features.

In studying a collection of images, the arrangement of images actively shapes the analytical process, in that a display technique could enable a particular interpretive avenue (and foreclose others). The point of departure is that visual models are not innocent but embed specific forms of knowledge (Drucker, 2014). Similarly, the arrangement of images collates a display format with a particular method of analysis, connecting 'design decisions and methodological reasoning' (Borra & Rieder, 2014). Each distinctive way of arranging a collection of images allows a unique analytical procedure. The question is which arrangement suits a particular analysis (and not others). It is also important to note that sometimes display formats look similar, but the processing of the images (i.e., the organizing logic) is done differently. For example, as illustrated below, one can cluster images by colour hue or by means of more sophisticated computer vision-assisted techniques that also consider image content. The result will look the same but should be interpreted differently.

In the context of digital research, the most straightforward way to arrange a collection of images is by retaining the order provided by the platform. For example, when working with search engine results, one would display images retaining their ranking as they appear on the results page. When working with social media content, one could array images shared with a particular hashtag, displaying them from top to bottom according to their engagement metrics. The display format often used in these instances is a grid-like visualization, where columns represent different (hashtag or otherwise demarcated) spaces and images in each column can be read from top to bottom in descending order of engagement (or ranking). Displaying images using platforms' rankings serves particularly well in studying the resonance of various issues, asking how far a particular issue appears from the top of search engine results. For example, one queries a search engine for the term [climate change] and, retaining images in the order returned in the search, observes how far from the top activism-related images appear vis-à-vis content that downplays or denies the problem.

When working with display formats that repurpose platform rankings, it is helpful to code images visually to ease the observation of how close particular types of content are from the top of the source (in terms of ranking). In one example, researchers have displayed images from the query 'RFID' in Google Images (Rogers, 2018a) and overlaid those that indicate a 'wet' association of the technology (such as with humans or animals) with an icon, as opposed to images that represent 'dry' associations (packaging and circuit boards). Generally, retaining the platform's order in the display format allows researchers to study platforms themselves alongside their visual content, in a form of visual research that keeps together media and issue research (as one makes findings about the resonance of a particular issue as well as studying platform-specific ways of ranking and indexing content). Chapter 3 is dedicated to approaches that focus on this type of research, where the ranking logics of social media platforms and search engines are made an important object of study, together with images and their visual content. In this chapter, instead, we focus on research strategies that seek to re-order image sets following other criteria, such as their colours or contents.

Image colour maps: grouping images by formal similarity

One way into a large collection of images is to group them by formal property and organize them into the space accordingly. Depending on the software one uses for the task, the output may change slightly, with images displayed as a grid, cluster map (similar to a network graph), or scatterplot (having two distinct features mapped on the two axes). Generally, images are clustered based on their formal properties (such as hue, lightness, and saturation) in order to have similar images close in the visualization.

The computational analysis of formal features has been initially explored with large sets of digitized artworks. In a Cultural Analytics approach (Manovich, 2020), one compares the entire body of work of two artists and makes findings about their 'footprints' (Manovich, 2011c). In one example, two sets of paintings (from competing artists such as Mondrian and Rothko or van Gogh and Gauguin) are displayed on a coordinate space according to measured formal features (i.e., brightness, hue, or saturation). The output enables a comparison of the visual choices of the two painters, with one, say, using a brighter colour spectrum and the other exploring a broader range of colour hues.

The analysis of images' formal features can be the endpoint (as is the case with the examples above) or instrumental to other research goals. One may cluster images by formal similarity not so much to make findings about it, but to identify copies and variations of the same image and quantify their prominence in a collection at a glance. The technique allows for grouping similar images and copies of the same image and may be used to understand how images are modified when circulating. It enables distant reading of a large collection but also lends itself to the close inspection of smaller groups, as similar images are inspected and subsequently analysed. For example, the technique has been used to distil visual genres in UK tabloids' images posted on social media (Generic Visuals in the News Team, 2022). Here, clustering enables the researcher to form groups of similar images, which are inspected closely, and named according to their visual characteristics, such as front page, breaking news alert, quote card, and question card, among others.

Another example is a study of the images shared with #parisagreement on Instagram before and after Donald Trump announced his plan to withdraw the United States from the Paris Agreement, signed one year earlier by over 195 states at the UN Conference of the Parties. With the help of software, images from the two periods are displayed on a grid and grouped by similarity in colour. The two sets of images (before and after the announcement), presented side by side, reveal the tremendous increase in image-sharing activity for this particular hashtag, as the grid on the left (compiling images from an earlier time frame) is considerably smaller than the one on the right (figure 2.2). As the visualization shows, the impact of Trump's announcement results in heightened activity around the topic of climate change, and, in particular, around the subtopic of the Paris Agreement. But the visualization also offers a direct way to the data set, as one can spot dominant formats by looking at the large clusters of similarly coloured images. For example, in the right grid (which compiles images shared after Donald Trump's withdrawal), the most visible and more prominent cluster is made up of light blue images, corresponding to copies and slight variations of the same graphic image 'Make Our Planet Great Again', launched by French President Emmanuel Macron in reaction to the Trump announcement.

The output is a form of direct visualization (Manovich, 2011b) as it shows the entire image collection, allowing researchers to review and rearrange the actual materials without translating them into, for instance, diagrammatic shapes or schemes. The zoom out is also a form of distant reading as it allows researchers to spot patterns (such as repetition in formats) that would be hard to observe by browsing through the images in a folder.

#parisagreement   one month after 1/6/17 - 20:36

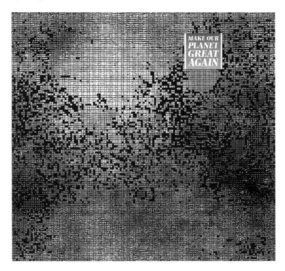

one month before
1/6/17 20:36

1.203 images   14.395 images

2.2 Images posted with #parisagreement on Instagram before and after Donald Trump announced the withdrawal of the United States from the Paris Agreement on 1 June 2017.

Image clusters: grouping images by content with computer vision

Computer vision can also be used to group images. Here, one clusters and visualizes images in a collection according to how machine learning algorithms classify their content. With this approach, images are clustered if they are categorized as similar by a computer-vision algorithm. In the output, usually a cluster map, spatial proximity is a function of (content) similarity, as images that share similar features are grouped together. The approach may be used to detect thematic visual clusters and quantify their volume visually inside a collection of images. The technique also yields marginal, smaller, or disconnected thematic groups of images. It works well for exploratory analysis of the visual representations of an issue, as groups are graphically demarcated, named, and investigated further.

The technique generally consists of two steps, whether produced with a chain of tools or stand-alone software. First, images are classified with the help of a computer-vision API (application programming interface). Second, the result of the classification is used to arrange images so that similarly classified ones are displayed closer to each other in the visualization. Like other forms of multidimensional data (and connected visualization), such as network graphs, it produces a 'good enough' space (Perez & Tah, 2020), whose ambiguity requires researchers to adopt an active research attitude. The topological visual ambiguity of the display (Venturini et al., 2021) aligns well with exploratory work, lending itself to multiple visual entry points and a loose exploration of clusters.

There are limits to repurposing computer vision for digital research. Despite its power of seeing at scale, therefore allowing researchers to expand the number of materials to analyse, computer vision may lack the ability to grasp the meaning of networked images, and additional platform data (such as comments, hashtags, and likes) might be needed to account for the complex meaning-making processes around images online (Geboers & Van De Wiele, 2020). Another critique often raised against the computational analysis of large groups of images refers to the flaws and shortcomings of computer vision tools – in particular, concerning issues of racial and gender representation (Buolamwini & Gebru, 2018; Crawford & Paglen, 2019; Sinders, 2020) – due to the limits of the training sets behind them.

While being aware of its limits and shortcomings, computer vision can be used to support the analysis of large collections of images. In the case of social media images, grouping with computer vision helps to detect recurrent visual themes and dominant media formats in a set of images. It may also render marginal themes visible as one evaluates the size of one cluster of similar images compared to others. The approach has been used for exploratory work into the online imagery associated with a place, such as the city of Paris (Stefaner, 2018); to study visual content related to a sports event (D'Andréa & Mints, 2019); to examine visual (online and offline) practices concerning a protest movement (Stepnik et al., 2020); or for studying the visual *issue-fication* of an environmental incident such as wildfires (D'Andréa & Mints, 2021). When applied to multiple image collections, one can use the method to compare competing visual spaces, building on 'programme and anti-programme research' (Rogers, 2017), such as pro-impeachment vs anti-coup content concerning the Brazilian president Dilma Rousseff on Instagram (Omena et al., 2020), or topical vs sentimental hashtag spaces in relation to the Syrian war on Twitter (Geboers & Van De Wiele, 2020).

It is important to note that the labelling and subsequent clustering of images is not the endpoint of the analysis, even though it may be when the technique is geared towards auditing purposes of the computer vision infrastructure itself. In this case, one could arrange the content of a training data set (Karpathy, 2014) to evaluate its diversity (or lack thereof) or cluster the inter-mediate steps of the machine interpretive process (i.e., network activations) to disclose how it represents different concepts (Carter et al., 2019). Instead, when employed for the exploratory study of social media images, labelling and clustering should mainly be considered research tools in support of interpretive moves: clusters of images are formed thanks to the affinity of computer vision labels but are then analysed and interpreted by the researcher. One can also consider opening up such interpretive processes to different publics (as we come back to in chapter 4).

In a project concerned with the online mapping of the issue of urban nature in the city of Paris (Ricci et al., 2017), images shared on Twitter with keywords such as 'nature', 'biodiversity', and 'urban agriculture' are analysed with computer vision. The outputs stimulate the observation of content-based clusters by displaying similar images close to each other (figure 2.3). First, an image content recognition algorithm generates a set of descriptive tags for each image. Then, a network of images and tags is created and used to determine the position of each image in the final output (where tags are removed and images retained). Clusters are then collaboratively interpreted and annotated in a collective interpretation exercise. The results of the collaborative analysis (i.e., annotated image clusters) are then summarized in a diagram. The process foregrounds dominant and marginal visual themes, such as the lack of human presence in the represen-tation of nature or the selective presence of certain animals (and the absence of others) in the discourse about biodiversity. The technique also brings to the fore visual clichés used to discuss urban nature-related issues, such as the green wall and the green rooftop.

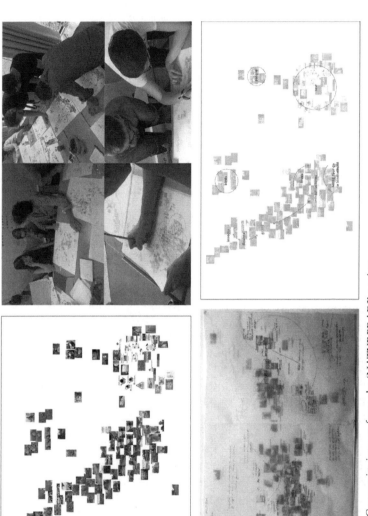

2.3 Composite images from the 'NATURPRADI' project.

Image timelines: displaying images by time

One other application of the distant-reading approach is to display images chronologically, repurposing temporal metadata such as timestamps. In this approach, images would be arranged according to when they are shared, either in a grid-like display or plot (with one additional dimension). Image timelines enable the study of patterns of image sharing over time, as one can appreciate the volume of images shared in different moments and detect similar images across the time frame under analysis. The technique fits well with the study of events online (and offline), such as protests, revolutions, or elections, in the tradition of 'remote event analysis' (Rogers, 2019, p. 167), where one displays online content chronologically to create an account of the event. The output is then narrative in nature, as one can follow a story unfolding over time. As the timeline also enables one to spot waves of similar images (or copies), one can also perform issue commitment analysis with it – that is, asking 'for how long is an issue a matter of concern to the actors?' (Rogers, 2018c, p. 459).

In a project studying the visual representation of a protest march on Twitter (Colombo & Azzi, 2016), the question is: which content – and for how long – is shared, beyond the usual 'riot porn' (Razsa, 2014)? Images shared with a set of hashtags are collected (together with timestamps) and subsequently arranged in a grid-like timeline from top to bottom. The timeline enables distant reading of the content shared throughout the day, as one can identify 'waves' of similar images shared at a particular moment and visually evaluate their sheer volume. As with other similar techniques, colours and formal features offer a rough way into the content (e.g., dark and red areas signalling a set of images depicting fire, white areas hinting at a group of flyers), but the analysis follows with the observation of individual images from each 'wave', selected from the entire image set.

Image timelines can also expose the lack of diversity in a set of images, as displaying them from old to new can show their homogeneity over time. One example is a study of the development of the visual representation of climate change, according to Google Image Search (Pearce & De Gaetano, 2021). Here, researchers collect images over a twelve-year time span from

Google Image Search and place them on a grid according to ranking (from top to bottom) and time (from left to right). The timeline (figure 2.4) exposes the lack of evolution in the visual representation of climate change (according to Google Search), which stays roughly identical over the time frame under analysis, with a notable absence of humans and the abundance of typical visual clichés, such as the earth on fire or the 'before and after' trope contrasting deserted and lush landscapes.

Image networks: grouping images by digital features

Another technique for distant reading of image sets is in the domain of relational analysis, specifically image networks. With image network analysis, one seeks to study how images are associated with other digital objects, such as hashtags, emojis, keywords, or reactions. It builds on the networked nature of digital images (Niederer, 2018), focusing on how images in the online realm are linked to digital objects such as hashtags, users, and platforms. The point of departure is that these elements concur in shaping the meaning of digital images and thus should be included in the analysis.

The preferred output is a co-occurrence network map, where images and other digital objects are arranged in the same visualization so that those most used together are placed close to each other. In the analysis, clusters are statistically calculated (as one would do with visual network analysis), demarcated, named, and inspected further.

Clustering by shared hashtags enables a type of image audience research that seeks to identify 'hashtags publics' (Rambukkana, 2015) and their distinctive visualities. Which types of images (and publics that share them) cluster around a set of hashtags? What visual materials are shared by those in favour of shale gas extraction compared to those that advocate against it (Rabello et al., 2021)? A study found a correlation between the actor's standpoints in the controversy and the type of image used (photographs of people, infographics, landscapes, images of protesters).

In another similar study, researchers asked how the land is visually constructed by actors with different stances towards

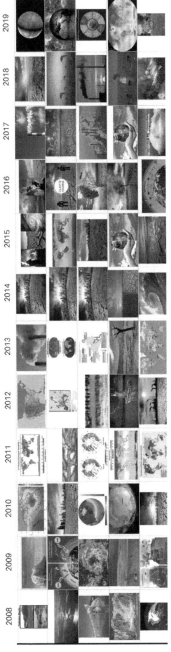

2.4 A ranked image timeline showing the top five Google Image results per year for the query 'climate change'. Source: Pearce & De Gaetano (2021).

the construction of Canada's controversial Trans Mountain pipeline (Karsgaard & MacDonald, 2020). Two image–hashtag networks, the pro- and anti-pipeline, illustrate two visually distinct ways of depicting the land (as a resource commodity vs as an object for conservation).

Another example of an image–hashtag network pertains to Twitter – specifically a study of images shared on Twitter during the 2019 Amazon forest fires (Bounegru et al., 2022). The analysis visualizes the relationships between images and hashtags associated with misinformation (e.g., #fakenews and #hoax) to see which specific types of images circulated with misinformation hashtags. The relationship between images and hashtags offers an overview of how different image formats animate different debates regarding misinformation on the Amazon fires. The image–hashtag network reveals affinities among hashtags and images, which compose distinct clusters of visual misinformation-related practices. One is 'screenshot debunking', where screenshots of other tweets or news articles debunking misinformation around the Amazon rainforest fires, in particular about the sharing of recycled images which could mislead, are shared with hashtags such as #fakenews and #misinformation. One other is using memes to mock misinformation practices, specifically sharing recycled and potentially misleading images about the fires. These are highly exaggerated 'fake' images of animals (e.g., dolphins and dinosaurs) in danger because of the fires, in a sort of commentary, performed through memes, of the Amazon fires as a visual misinformation issue.

The networkedness of digital images also opens up research avenues for studying affective publics assembled through shared sentiment, opinion, or affect (Papacharissi, 2014). Studying the ways in which such publics react to images online provides new insights into the visual user cultures of a particular platform (Geboers et al., 2020). Studying associations between images and hashtag is one application of image network analysis. Another would be the study of the affective dimension of digital images with reactions (used on Facebook to engage with content). Which reactions (a shortcut for sentiment) are most likely associated with which images? In a project studying posts about the Syrian war on Facebook (Geboers et al., 2020), a network graph shows the uneven distribution of images across reactions. In figure 2.5, images are clustered around Facebook reactions,

love   sad   angry

2.5 A bipartite network of the distribution of posted images across Facebook Reactions (detail). Source: Geboers et al. (2020).

with the sad reaction visibly bigger than the others (as it is used more frequently). The visualization shows how sad and angry reactions are primarily used together and often with images depicting children. In contrast, soldiers and sign-holding activists are found to be more associated with the love reaction. The study of the association of reactions and images, operationalized with an image network, allows researchers to infer 'collective attitudes and performative emotional expressions' in relation to the visuals of the war (Geboers et al., 2020).

Clustering images by web pages also enables circulation research, as one studies the kind of images that travel in different online spaces. This approach puts forward the 'site of circulation' (Rose, 2016) as one crucial location where images produce meaning and may be interpreted. How and where does a set of images travel online? How are images modified, re-contextualized, and transformed while travelling across different web spaces? Here the output is similar to image–hashtag networks, but the network is built by leveraging the connection between images and web pages (focusing on top-level domains) where they are found. One example is a study of images returned on Google Search with the query 'climate emergency' (Omena et al., 2021). The image–domain network allows a kind of source critique driven by visual material, where one evaluates which domains share the same or similar visual content and those hosting distinct types of images.

Ethical considerations for displaying images in visual research

While crafting visualizations of images (as we illustrate in this chapter and the following ones) for analytical purposes and as research outputs shared in publications and presentations, it is essential to take time for an ethical consideration of whether or not to display the original images in the final outputs. Particularly when researching sensitive topics, one should consider implementing strategies to ensure anonymity and make personal details unrecognizable. As these concerns have been addressed in social media research for some time, different approaches have been explored to respect users' privacy expectations. However, the task might be thornier when research deals with visual content – in which the visualization formats are such an essential part of the research process.

Nevertheless, there are some strategies that researchers can put in place to respect users' right to privacy and ensure anonymity when dealing with visual content. Zooming out in itself, which in this chapter we present as a technique to perform distant reading of collections of online images, can also become a method to protect privacy: reproducing images at a small scale prevents re-identification or reverse look-up of low-resolution images, which become too small to be appreciated and traced back to their original versions (see, for example, Marres et al., 2023). Filters and various image-editing techniques (such as blurring or stylizing filters that turn photographic images into line drawings, for example, by showing only silhouettes) can also be used to make personal details unrecognizable from reproduced images while still conveying the overall composition of the original photo (Tiidenberg & Baym, 2017; Sánchez-Querubín, 2020).

Concerning obfuscation techniques that involve hiding, blurring, or anonymizing data, an argument has been made that these strategies are no longer enough when researchers act in 'increasingly public, archivable, searchable, and traceable spaces' (Markham, 2012). In the realm of social media research with textual data, there have been calls for more creative techniques for disguising details about the individuals being studied. One example is 'fabrication', which involves 'creative, bricolage-style transfiguration of original data into composite accounts' (Markham, 2012, p. 334) or even crafting fictional dialogues and stories that would hinder the possibility of tracing back the data to their sources. Following the notion of fabrication as an ethical practice, one could think of similar strategies tailored explicitly to visual content. One option would be to take a more drastic approach than simply blurring or editing individual images and *craft* image collages starting from fragments of original ones. One more extreme procedure could entail resorting to generative visual artificial intelligence (AI) to recreate alternative versions – which could be seen as illustrations – of (some or all) images in the data set. The newly generated visuals would be similar to the original ones (in terms of composition, colours, and styles), but they would partially protect the right to anonymity of the owners of the original images.

Conclusion

This chapter starts with a room full of printed photographs. In the art installation, visitors walk through a valley of images filling up the space and can pick up images to inspect them closer. While the task might be overwhelming to some, in the photo we have chosen, a boy is smiling as he looks at one picture he has picked up from the ground. This chapter presents methods for navigating the multiplicity of digital images using visual methods while still paying attention to the specificity of individual images.

The approaches to image analysis explored in this chapter build on two key aspects. First, they involve analysing image sets from a distance, which allows for the identification of visual patterns. Second, they focus on collections of images as the primary research object and enable researchers to examine multiple images together. Custom (or tool-assisted) display formats arrange images in a particular configuration to support their analytical interpretation. The distant-reading attitude is not the endpoint of the research process, but it is a (often preliminary) step that allows the analysis of visual patterns among image sets, as well as pinpointing individual images that require further scrutiny. Display formats are crucial in this move from the distant to the close view. By rearranging, re-ordering, and structuring images into particular formations, the researcher can deal with the multiplicity of images in a collection and also focus on individual images.

This approach to image analysis is particularly well suited for answering a range of research questions. For example, it can be used to identify recurring visual formats and themes within a collection of images, including the analysis of these patterns over time. Additionally, the distant approach can help researchers to analyse repetitions and modifications of images, including poor images (those that are copied and circulated or resulting from memetic practices). Furthermore, it allows for the analysis of the relationship between images and other digital objects (such as hashtags or reactions) when the arrangement of image sets is driven by shared digital features, and may enable researchers to study how visual content circulates online.

In using the techniques presented in this chapter, one often resorts to tools for the analysis (and subsequent arrangement) of different image features. From computer vision algorithms to software for the analysis of colours, one should approach such tools with a critical stance, making their operations part of the object of study. In particular, one should not take for granted the kinds of associations these tools produce, aware of how such automatisms often generate inequalities based on power imbalances and carry multiple biases. In chapter 4, we address these issues by exploring how visual research can be used to study bias in the visual representation of various issues in the digital realm.

Although we present zooming out as a means to detect overall patterns and then reach individual images, approaching large image sets may shift the focus away from the specificity of single images. In addition, even if some display formats use digital objects to arrange images (such as image–hashtag networks), this chapter does not explicitly address platforms' roles in co-producing content. The following chapter introduces methods that involve careful consideration of online networks' role in determining the presentation, ranking, and creation of digital images: chapter 3 is dedicated to techniques for analysing small groups of images in detail, focusing on their networked nature and on the influence of online platforms in shaping and distributing visual content.

Further Readings

- boyd, danah & Crawford, K. (2011). Six provocations for Big Data. *SSRN Electronic Journal*. doi.org/10.2139/ssrn.1926431.
- Colombo, G., Bounegru, L. & Gray, J. (2023). Visual models for social media image analysis: groupings, engagement, trends, and rankings. *International Journal Of Communication*, 17, 28. https://ijoc.org/index.php/ijoc/article/view/18971.
- Manovich, L. (2020). *Cultural Analytics*. Cambridge, MA: MIT Press.

3

Networked Images: Platform Image Analysis

This chapter introduces techniques for close-reading small sets of images. It demonstrates methods for studying multiple issues on a single platform in a single language, or a single issue across multiple platforms and languages. It ends by comparing various visualization methods for small image collections.

Introduction

In a tweet from 2017, Arnold Schwarzenegger holds a cut-out sign with the text #MakeOurPlanetGreatAgain (figure 3.1). The phrase – a wordplay on Donald Trump's campaign slogan 'Make America Great Again' – refers to a slogan (and graphic) shared by Emmanuel Macron in response to the US withdrawal from the Paris Agreement. The tweet is an example of how images may be networked online. In the text, hashtags and mentions link the image to other tweets and users – in this case, directly addressing @EmmanuelMacron, and using the hashtag #COP23 to connect the tweet to the 2017 United Nations Climate Change Conference in Bonn. In response, other users have connected the image and their accounts by liking or retweeting the post

User who posted ⟶

Mentioned user ⟶

⟵ **Hashtags**

⟵ **Users who liked this**

Date and time ⟶

Retweets and likes ⟶

Comments ⟶

3.1 Screenshot of a tweet by Arnold Schwarzenegger, annotated to show how content is networked by users and by the platform itself.

or leaving a comment. In addition, the platform itself adds a timestamp and thus connects the image to the other images posted at that same date and time.

This chapter introduces methods for close-reading small sets of images, with a sensitivity towards their networked nature and the role of online platforms in ranking, formatting, and co-producing (visual) content. In the field of visual studies, one can find a variety of methods relying on 'close engagement with specific images' (Rose, 2016). From visual semiotics to compositional analysis and visual rhetoric, from discourse analysis to visual framing analysis, the developing (yet fragmented) field of visual studies offers a variety of methods that promote an 'attentive stance' (Rose, 2016) towards the material under analysis. For the close reading of small sets of online images, we draw from content analysis, albeit amended to cater to the specific networked nature of digital images. Content analysis, developed in communication science and known for its unobtrusive methods and inclusive approach to all content types (text, image, sound, and audiovisual), is often associated with quantitative approaches to the collecting and counting of recurring themes in media materials. However, content analysis, as theorized by Klaus Krippendorff, has moved from its 'shallow counting game, motivated by a journalistic fascination with numbers and a narrow conception of science in which quantitative measurements provided the only evidence that counted' to 'redirect their attention to social phenomena that are both generated by and constituted in texts and images and, hence, [need] to be understood through their written and pictorial manifestations' (Krippendorff, 2018, p. xii).

In reaction to the multiple and dispersed approaches to researching (with) visual materials (e.g., Prosser, 1998; Van Leeuwen & Jewitt, 2001; Bell, 2004; Pink, 2012; Mannay, 2016; Banks, 2018; Aiello & Parry, 2020), there have been taxonomic projects for evaluating visual methods. One approach is to cluster methods by 'sites of meaning' – distinguishing between the study of the production, circulation, and audiencing of images – and evaluate methods according to their suitability to tackle each site where images may produce and generate meaning (Rose, 2016). From this perspective, concerns have been raised in relation to content analysis of the visual, described as a technique focusing exclusively on image content as a site for meaning, not having 'much purchase' (Rose, 2016, p. 103) on the sites of image circulation, audiencing, or production. Networked content analysis, as discussed below, counters these concerns by including the study of online image carriers (e.g., digital platforms), their technical features, and user engagement, which are studied together with the image content itself.

Networked content analysis as a digital method

The presented approach to networked content analysis is based on two main principles. First, online content is primarily accessed and structured through search engines and platforms. Second, the technical nature of the content should be integrated into its analysis. This approach calls for content analysis methods that account for the unique characteristics of each platform and understand how content moves within these platforms. The goal is to ensure a deep understanding of content in its native digital context. Therefore, networked content analysis can be understood as a digital method.[5]

Content analysis has traditionally been applied to various visual data sets, such as a collection of prime-time television broadcasts, photographs in newspaper articles on a particular topic, or a set of comic books (Krippendorff, 2018). Online visual content, however, exists in and through the platforms and engines that produce it. This difficulty of demarcating online content as it circulates online has been described as following a moving target through a microscope by media and communications scholar Sally McMillan, who proposed to standardize methods to stabilize the approach (Niederer, 2019; McMillan, 2000). In response, linguist and communications scholar Susan Herring proposed to combine traditional content analysis techniques with methodologies from disciplines such as linguistics and sociology to offer a more workable response to the challenges offered by 'new online media' (Herring, 2010; Niederer, 2019).

Digital images can be placed with a news article networked through in-text hyperlinks, or recommendations to similar articles, or pulled into social media using social media buttons (Gerlitz & Helmond, 2013; Niederer, 2019). The networked nature of online content and its entanglement with the hosting platforms entails analytical sensitivity that recognizes that each platform handles and serves content differently. For instance, search engines serve results in a ranked list, Wikipedia cleans and organizes its content with bots, Twitter links one post to another through hashtags and comments, and Tiktok suggests content to users based on a highly sophisticated personalization algorithm.

The technological specificities of online platforms mean that a clean separation of content from its carrier is no longer feasible, and urge the researcher to move beyond content analysis alone and treat the particular content technicities as part of the object of study. In this chapter, we illustrate a version of content analysis adapted to the networked nature of digital images. Networked content analysis (Niederer, 2019) emphasizes the technicity of digital content. Technicity refers to the technologically composed nature of web content that can hardly be separated from its carrier (a specific web platform, for instance) and points out that technical agents such as hyperlinks and shares are not mere features but part of the content under study.

In this chapter, we illustrate how networked content analysis, applied to the study of small collections of digital images, can answer diverse research questions. Firstly, we look at techniques for single-platform visual analysis, demonstrating how one can study multiple issues by comparing images from one platform. Secondly, we turn to cross-cultural visual analysis, where one repurposes language-specific features of social media platforms and search engines to analyse cultural specificities in the representation of various issues. Thirdly, we move to cross-platform visual analysis, introducing techniques to study platform visual vernaculars. The chapter ends by reviewing the different visualization methods and display modes that support this type of research.

Single-platform visual analysis: studying multiple issues on a single platform

Social media platforms offer possibilities for the visual analysis of multiple issues. When studying images from a single platform, one often starts by repurposing technical features and platform-specific affordances (such as hashtags, engagement metrics, and interaction scores) to demarcate small collections of images (and their associated features). After data collection, images are usually displayed following their digital features (e.g., ranked from most to least interacted with) and inspected closely. In analysing the collected images, a networked approach entails considering each image as part of a larger set of (visual and non-visual) elements such as captions, hashtags, the users posting, and the users mentioned in captions and comments. Sensitivity to the networked nature of visual content means including all these contextual elements in the analysis and not focusing only on the image's content.

In traditional content analysis, researchers devise a coding scheme as an analytical lens through which to read the collection of images or compare multiple image collections. An exhaustive coding scheme would allow for typical content analysis research questions, such as 'questions of bias: comparative questions about the duration, frequency, priority or salience of representations of, say, political personalities, issues, policies, or of "positive" versus "negative" features of representation' (Bell, 2004, p. 14). A content analysis begins with formulating a research question (and often a hypothesis) and, subsequently, the compilation of an (exhaustive) list of (mutually exclusive) variables and their possible values. The researcher conducting the analysis will focus on the 'manifest content', meaning that they will focus on what is represented rather than on 'reality' (the example given by Bell is that when someone is shown to play an elderly person, that is what the researcher classifies, and not the actual age of the actor) (Bell, 2004, pp. 15–16).

Depending on the research question, it may be most fruitful not to predefine the variables and values but, instead, employ emergent coding to capture the specific *issue language* of various actors and sources as they resonate online. Rather than using predefined categories or translating jargon into more familiar terms, this approach aspires to *follow the actors* in their own words.

Content analysis and – attuned to online research – networked content analysis allow for the study of the salience and resonance of particular types of images (and their accompanying text) as they circulate online, within and across platforms and engines. In what follows, we illustrate single-platform visual analysis focusing on Instagram, which is currently 'most associated with online images' (Rogers, 2021, p. 1), but the approach might also be deployed to other platforms. In particular, we focus on Instagram as a site interested in information disorders (Bounegru et al., 2018), such as misinformation and polarization, before and after elections.

Studying problematic information on Instagram

Though Facebook has been labelled the 'fake news machine' (Herrman, 2016) and Twitter studied as a matter of routine, owing to the availability of data sets, Instagram, when scrutinized, has been found to perform well as an outlet for junk or hyperpartisan news circulation, artificially amplified engagement, and other types of problematic content. Instagram is also increasingly discussed as a site for misinformation and polarization, particularly in connection with politically charged issues such as the COVID-19 pandemic, vaccines, or gun regulation. As a case in point, under the guise of wellness and lifestyle posts, conspiracy and anti-vax content are transformed into gradient pastel images presented to a willing audience. Furthermore, since it is a platform designed around sharing visual materials, Instagram may be well suited for the so-called 'image-centric memetic (meme) warfare' (New Knowledge, 2018, p. 8) – that is, the weaponized use of image macros to stir conflict and foster division online.

In one example, the focus is on the circulation of junk content in high-engagement political spaces on Instagram during the 2019 Dutch provincial and European parliamentary elections (figure 3.2) (Colombo & De Gaetano, 2020). The study aims to analyse engaging content in Dutch political spaces on Instagram and observe how much engagement is generated by content that can be characterized as disinformation, conspiracy, clickbait, hyperpartisan, or satirical. As a first step, the study outlines the Dutch political space on Instagram by collecting images from the platform that are posted with a list of hashtags concerning political parties and personalities (e.g., #markrutte), as well as politically charged issues such as climate change (e.g., #klimaatverandering). For each hashtag, a set of Instagram posts shared in the run-up to the Dutch elections is collected, together with their metadata (date of the post, media URL, caption, number of comments, and number of likes). Subsequently, posts

3.2 Twenty most-liked posts per hashtag shared around the 2019 Dutch provincial elections, sorted from the right (most junk) to the left (least junk). Source: Colombo & De Gaetano (2020).

are filtered based on engagement metrics (retaining only the twenty most-liked posts per hashtag), and unrelated content and identical posts are filtered out.

The analysis starts with displaying each hashtag-related image collection in dedicated columns, in which the posts are also ranked from the most liked in the first row to the least liked one in the last. It follows with the close reading of post captions and embedded media (images and videos) to understand how political party leaders and politically charged topics are discussed within the limits of the Instagram Dutch political space, and specifically to flag the presence of junk content. To characterize the type of content associated with each hashtag, an image staining technique (Rogers, 2021) is applied to the grid of posts, which involves juxtaposing a different coloured stripe next to the posts that may be characterized as problematic (e.g., disinformation, hyperpartisan, conspiracy, clickbait, or satirical). In the output, one can note the amount of the different kinds of problematic content (according to the coding scheme) at a glance and its placement, as posts are ranked from most to least liked.

The analysis yields general results (as one visually evaluates the number of posts juxtaposed with colour, characterized as problematic ones) and hashtag-specific ones (as not all image sets present the same amount of flagged content). The study found a relative scarcity of junk content in the demarcated high-engagement political Dutch space. Moreover, the majority of the posts flagged as junk can be considered hyperpartisan, primarily supporting or opposing particular ideologies or figures, while only one post can be considered clickbait and one conspiracy-related. The findings also suggest that specific issues, such as the Zwarte Piet debate, and particular political leaders, including Geert Wilders, leader of the right-wing populist Party for Freedom, draw more divisive content than others. In general, the study did not find evident signs of dubiousness in the most-liked content around the 2019 European elections, except for a few hyperpartisan posts. In conclusion, while problematic content may have been circulated during that time, this study finds that such content did not receive the most engagement on Instagram.

A subsequent study on the quality of information around elections on Instagram shifts attention to the 2020 US presidential elections (Niederer & Colombo, 2023). Here, the focus is on posts that receive the most user interactions concerning the US presidential candidates of 2020, the COVID-19 pandemic, and a selection of particularly controversial campaign issues (such as healthcare, 5G, and gun control). The research protocol joins data collection that repurposes Instagram-specific features (hashtags and interaction scores) with a coding scheme attuned to online content's ambiguous nature. Data collection is operationalized by compiling a list of keywords for each candidate, including candidate names, campaign slogans, and most-used hashtags by candidate supporters. In addition, a list of terms referring to the most-mentioned topics in the candidate spaces (healthcare, COVID-19, 5G, and gun control) is also compiled, paying attention to including official terms, vernacular words, and, if applicable, pro- and counter- terminology (e.g., by including in the query both the term 'gun control' and 'gun ownership'). For each query, fifty posts are retained based on the total sum of their interactions, which is the number of likes and comments by Instagram users that a post has received.

After manually removing unrelated posts from the data set, the process follows with the close reading of the top fifty posts per space, considering both the visual elements (image or video) and the post captions. Each post is analysed by applying a four-category analytical scheme, which considers the content's divisiveness and ambiguity. Posts that fuel conflict, polarization, or even radicalization are flagged as divisive (following Benkler et al., 2018), in contrast to more positive messages (e.g., supporting a candidate or sharing quarantine tips), which are labelled as non-divisive. Following Phillips and Millner (2017), 'ambivalent content' is contrasted with 'earnest content' to categorize posts that are not inflammatory per se but may still generate a lighter form of division by possibly excluding those who do not have the cultural references to decode it, laugh about it, and, involuntarily, become 'laughed at' (Phillips & Millner, 2017). In opposition to 'earnest and non-divisive' content, inflammatory posts that might fuel polarization, conspiracy, or conflict are categorized as 'earnest and divisive'. Content that is not inflammatory but may still generate a lighter form of division is categorized as 'ambivalent and non-divisive'. Finally, content that, while ambivalent, can be recognized as highly dismissive, violent, polarizing, or otherwise geared towards division is coded as 'ambivalent and divisive'.

The outcomes of the content analysis of the full set are visualised in a grid (figure 3.3), in which each horizontal row represents a distinct image collection concerning political candidates or issues. The posts are ranked from left to right, from those receiving the most to those getting the least user interactions, and colour-coded to represent the content category. This visualization offers an overview of the relative number of posts that can be considered divisive, earnest, or ambivalent and their position in the grid (which signifies their level of user engagement).

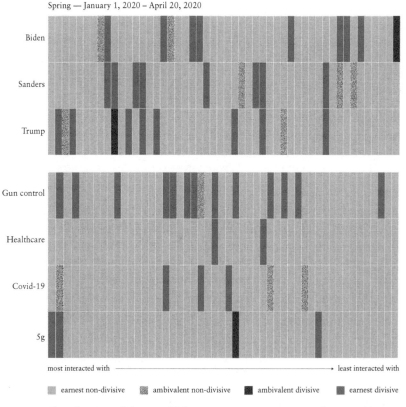

3.3 Classification of the top fifty Instagram posts (receiving the most interactions) in the political candidates' name spaces and issues spaces. Date range: 1 January 2020 – 20 April 2020. Visualized with Google Spreadsheet and Adobe Illustrator. Source: Niederer & Colombo (2023).

The study counterintuitively found Instagram to be a site of earnest political campaigning and moral support, with a relative lack of polarizing content and little to no misinformation. While social media platforms such as Instagram have been described as sites of misinformation and divisiveness, particularly around elections, in this study, however, the political and issue coverage that has received the most user interactions on Instagram from January to mid-April 2020 is primarily earnest and non-divisive, with scant ambivalent content. Concerning the political candidates, approximately 85 per cent of the posts are non-divisive, and the vast majority are earnest. The amount of divisiveness in each of the different candidates' name spaces is more or less the same, but nearly half of the divisive content found in the data set is posted by either Trump or Trump Jr, and most of the remaining divisive posts are about Trump.

The analysis then moves on by zooming into the role of influencers, including celebrities. By closely reading the most engaging posts, one can note that they mostly share responsible posts. For example, celebrities post supportive messages addressing care for one's mental health during a pandemic and encouraging people to vote. Another category shows how life (for celebrities, at least) continues despite the pandemic. Here, we find Kim Kardashian celebrating her fortieth birthday on a private island, and see how actor Dwayne Johnson, aka 'The Rock', arranged for the building of a replica of the Roman museum Castel Sant-Angelo as a film set, when travelling became impossible. Overall, the analysis finds a healthier platform than one might expect from a platform often associated with misinformation. While misinformation and polarization might be spreading on the platform, it receives little user interaction.

In this example, single-platform analysis with a theory-based coding scheme (rather than one based on variables and values), combined with a close reading of the most-engaging images, offered a closer look into the content and actors most present around certain social issues. Furthermore, it allowed for a classification of the most engaging content and the platform as a whole, resulting in the counter-intuitive finding that Instagram is an 'earnest' platform during polarizing events such as the election and the pandemic.

Cross-cultural image analysis:
comparing one issue across languages

While still on one platform, there are possibilities for comparisons. A networked approach to visual analysis might involve comparing images across language spaces to analyse cultural specificities. Here, one builds on the localization of digital platforms and search engines to map cultural biases and language preferences in the visual representation of one issue.

Wikipedia is the most straightforward platform for illustrating a networked approach to cross-cultural image analysis. The collaboratively written encyclopaedia project has been researched thoroughly in the realm of user-generated content and critically approached as 'a sociotechnical system' (Niederer & Van Dijck, 2010), wherein the technical structures and social hierarchies that govern the content creation process are foregrounded. Unique to Wikipedia (and other Wiki-based platforms) are its publicly accessible article editing histories (including automated edits by software robots), previous versions of each article, talk pages, and elaborate statistics, all opening up a rich research environment for the study of knowledge 'in the making' (Niederer & Van Dijck, 2010).

Wikipedians (as contributors to Wikipedia call themselves) try to avoid at all costs the occurrence of a dead end: an unlinked and isolated Wikipedia entry. No article should remain un-networked, and all entries should guide users to articles on the same topic in other languages, and related articles. Further, in-text links should be made to refer readers to dedicated articles and biographic entries of all people mentioned. All Wikipedia content, therefore, is or should be networked. This characteristic of the platform provides some powerful opportunities for researchers who are interested in studying cultural phenomena, such as the analysis of controversial (sub)topics with edits and discussion activity (Borra et al., 2015) or the analysis of communities of editors and their commitment to particular issues (Niederer & Van Dijck, 2010; Dijkstra & Krieg, 2016).

The different-language versions of one Wikipedia article enable a kind of visual research that seeks to study local (or language) visual vernaculars, as one can observe how issues are represented across the different-language chapters of a Wikipedia page. For example, researchers have studied images in the national versions of the Wikipedia page dedicated to the Srebrenica genocide – or massacre, according to the Serbian version (Rogers & Sendijarevic, 2012). The comparison of images contained in the different language versions (Serbian, Bosnian, Croatian, English, Dutch, and Serbo-Croatian), outputted with an image grid where each row represents one language, foregrounds cultural specificities in the visual account of the event, with a picture of a grave of a 13-year-old boy present in the Bosnian article but absent in the Serbian one.

Similarly, in a research project on the representation of art on Wikipedia, researchers compared the images in the article 'art' across all language versions of the encyclopaedia project (Kumar et al., 2013). This kind of research opens up important questions about both over- and under-representation of certain works of art in the writing and circulation of art history. Which artworks are shown across language versions and thus become the hard core of the Wikipedia art-historical canon (and, perhaps, even beyond)? Does Wikipedia privilege Western art, and are non-Western artists confined to a separate section in the entry? Which language versions succeed in striking a gender-balanced depiction of art? Which images have been on the art page for a long time, and which have been (recently) deleted or recently added to the articles? In the study, a network graph of artworks and language-specific pages shows how the 'Mona Lisa' has become 'the iconic representation of art itself' (Kumar et al., 2013) on Wikipedia, largely shared across pages. In some language versions (for example, the Icelandic, Corsican, and Hebrew pages), the 'Mona Lisa' was the only artwork presented in the entire article. The network also exposes language specificity, such as the Catalan page having a large set of unique artworks.

Wikipedia and its different language versions can be repurposed to study cultural and social phenomena, but cross-cultural (or cross-lingual) image analysis can also be performed with content from other online spaces. For instance, Google Image Search, and its local versions, can be repurposed to study cultural specificities in the visual representation of one issue. As a case in point, the art project 'The global anxiety monitor' (De Geuzen, 2006) juxtaposed live Google Image Search results for different languages. By querying 'anxiety buzzwords' (e.g., terrorism, epidemic, and financial crisis), each language delivers its own unique set of results, foregrounding differences and local specificities, such as the Palestinian National Liberation Movement logo uniquely returned by the Hebrew query for the term 'terrorism'.

More recently, the comparison of Google Image Search results has been automatized through a tool dubbed 'Search Atlas' (Ochigame & Ye, 2021), which programmatically displays juxtaposed grids of image results across countries. In the examples provided in figure 3.4, the query 'God' would return images following dominant national religions, and the query 'Tiananmen Square' would return the iconic photo of the 1989 protests in all languages, except for mainland China, where one could only find touristic and promotional images.

These examples each illustrate means to conduct comparative analysis within a single platform by looking at multiple issues on a single platform (in the example of Instagram described above), different language versions (e.g., Wikipedia), and different local versions (e.g., Google Image Search). Furthermore, single-platform analysis allows for the longitudinal analysis of how a

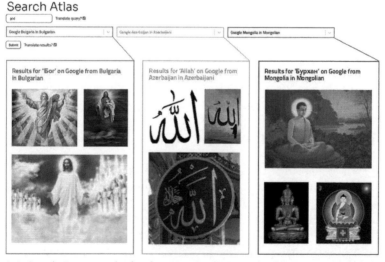

3.4 Google Image results for the query [god] in various languages and Google local domains.

platform 'performs' an issue over time – for instance, observing search engine results over time (see Pearce & De Gaetano, 2021, which we discussed in chapter 2). In addition, one could study how a single platform deals with controversy, as can be found, for example, in *Contropedia*, an effort to study contestation in issue-specific Wikipedia entries (Borra, 2023), and related studies of how Wikipedia resolves controversy (Niederer & van Dijck, 2010). In the next section, we will expand our scope to cross-platform analysis.

Cross-platform image analysis: studying platforms' visual vernaculars

After analysing multiple issues on a single platform and comparing one issue across languages, the following section introduces techniques for visual analysis across platforms. Moving from single-platform to cross-platform visual analysis is about 'uncollapsing' social media (Rogers, 2017) and attending to platform-sensitive affordances (Bucher & Helmond, 2018). A more apt term would be 'trans-platform analysis' (Rogers, 2017), following the differentiation made by Henry Jenkins between 'cross-media', where the same story is told across all platforms, and 'transmedia', where the story unfolds differently depending on the platform (Jenkins, 2006). The term hints at the special attention the researcher puts on the particular ways each platform has for 'formatting, prioritising, and recommending' (Niederer, 2018, p. 46) content and how these features are built into the analytical technique.

Indeed, cross-platform studies should start with 'a sensitivity to distinctive user cultures and subcultures' (Rogers, 2017) of each platform under examination. How are likes and shares used to boost content? Do hashtags work to connect content equally on Instagram or Twitter? The sensitivity required is towards users' practices and platforms' work. How does each platform amplify or demote content algorithmically? The extent to which a post is seen (in one's feed or as a result of a search query) is linked to (often opaque) 'ranking cultures' (Rieder et al., 2018, p. 52), a mix of ranking and recommendation mechanisms put in place by social media platforms. For instance, Instagram ranks content in feeds and stories based on several different 'signals', including information about the post, the user posting, and the user looking at the content (Mosseri, 2021). More practically, one should devise 'platform-specific data collection protocols' (Pearce et al., 2020, p. 168) to account for how various digital objects (e.g., likes, retweets, upvotes, shares, or views) work differently on various platforms.

Platform-specific affordances shape the emergence of particular visual styles and determine which visualities become 'elevated to prominence' (Geboers & Van De Wiele, 2020, p. 746). Comparing images across platforms may enable the study of such platform-specific visualities. With a general approach, one is after the most-shared image types on one platform, such as Twitter (Thelwall et al., 2016) or Instagram (Hu et al., 2014). In contrast, with issue-driven research (Marres, 2015b), one can study the platform-specific visual vernaculars of a given topic, asking how various platforms visually format an issue (Pearce et al., 2020). What is this topic about, according to Twitter or Instagram? Do they provide identical, similar, or distinct representations and descriptions of the same topic? The study of visual vernaculars approaches social media platforms as different windows onto an issue. Both approaches (the issue-driven and the issue-agnostic) require analysing and comparing images across platforms.

Visual vernaculars of climate change: image stacks

In one example, researchers looked at the visual representation of climate change (Niederer & Colombo, 2019; Pearce et al., 2020) across various online platforms and search engine results (i.e., Twitter, Facebook, Instagram, Google Image Search, and Reddit). The analysis focuses on high-engagement images to surface each platform's different *dominant* visual vernaculars. The process starts with defining platform-specific engagement and ranking metrics to filter and create subsets of 'most-engaged-with' images for the query [climate change]. Platform-specific cultures of use and distinctive user practices inform how to demarcate high-engagement images. For example, users employ comments and likes to engage with content on Instagram, while on Reddit users boost posts by 'upvoting'.

After data collection, images from each platform are aggregated in a new composite image (figure 3.5). Ten images per platform are ranked based on engagement level and layered on

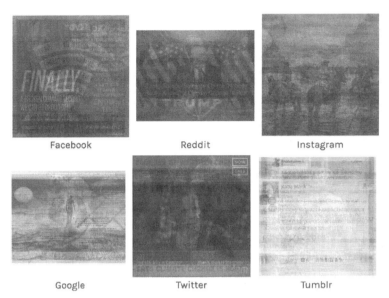

3.5 Image stacks to study platform visual vernaculars for the query [climate change]. Image courtesy of Beatrice Gobbo.

top of each other from most to least engaged with. The opacity of each image is lowered so that each of the ten images remains visible in the composite image. Each composite image offers a window into the styles and visual formats used to communicate climate change on each platform, helping to characterize each platform's distinctive style (or vernacular) in depicting the issue of climate change. As a platform built around image and aesthetics, Instagram presents text-free, professionally shot, and beautifully edited landscapes under pressure, which may be dubbed 'awareness traveling'. Images from Google Image Search are more hyperbolic in form and content with glaring and saturated colours, and depicted elements conform to the clichéd visual language of climate change (e.g., the polar bear and a picture of the Earth held in human hands). Tumblr offers 'environmental screenshotting': screenshots from other social media, such as Twitter, depicting iconic moments of the online climate change debate. Facebook presents 'shareable statements' about climate change: mainly non-controversial quotes, with large fonts, over photos of celebrities. Lastly, Reddit provides another distinct visual vernacular with trending news media content: 'press photo opportunities' with politicians behind microphones and national flags at the centre of each image.

Visual vernaculars of forest fires: an image grid

In another example (Colombo et al., 2023), the focus is on platform visual vernaculars (and their ranking) concerning the 2019 Amazon forest fires, one of the most globally mediatized rainforest fires of the recent past, in which viral images have played a prominent role in organizing worldwide public engagement (Madani, 2019; Weinberg, 2019). The study looks at the visual composition of the event in different online spaces. The process starts with collecting images from Twitter, Facebook, Instagram, Google Images, and YouTube through platform-specific queries. For example, on Twitter, where hashtags are employed to boost content, the data set is demarcated through hashtags such as #amazonfires or #prayforamazon; on platforms where hashtags are marginal (such as YouTube) or absent (such as Google Search), queries are adapted to become keywords.

In the visualization, each platform-specific image set is displayed as a grid (figure 3.6). The grid compares the top ten images per platform during the time frame under analysis, following platform-specific forms of engagement: most retweeted images on Twitter, the posts receiving the most interactions on Instagram and Facebook, most-viewed videos on YouTube, and highest-ranked images on Google Image Search. The grid of ranked images illustrates how each platform distinctively depicts the event: while Twitter shows the most diverse visual formats (including iconic photos, screenshots of other tweets, and video thumbnails), Google Images presents homogeneous visual imagery made of professional photographs of forest fires. YouTube has only images from mainstream news segments about the fires, prominently featuring the outlets' logos. On Facebook and Instagram, one old photo of burning forests tweeted by Emmanuel Macron dominates the space in various sizes and as a screenshot of tweets including it.

Cross-platform visualities emerge when one particular image (or type) recurs across columns. For example, Twitter screenshots are in several columns, denoting the centrality of the

Twitter   Instagram   Facebook   YouTube   Google

1st

10th

3.6 Top ten images per platform with English-language queries related to Amazon fires. Source: Colombo et al. (2023).

platform, whose content spills over into the others. In almost
all spaces, one can note a relative scarcity of images of
human actors, only marginally present on YouTube and Twitter:
responders, commentators, protesters, and rescuers are visible
– but not forest residents affected by the fires. The image grid
allows for critical inquiry into who and what is missing from
the data set and compares the results across issues, platforms,
or over time.

Conclusion

In this chapter, we presented approaches for the analysis of small
sets of networked images: studying the visual representation of
multiple issues on a single platform, comparing one issue across
language-versions of the same online space, and cross-platform
image analysis. While there are display modes for distant-
reading large collections of images (as discussed in chapter 2),
there are also preferred visualization modes for networked and
comparative visual analysis. As a way of conclusion, we discuss
various display formats that can be used to compare small
collections of networked images. In particular, we focus on two
main formats: the grid (where one arranges images in various
columns) and the stack (where images are instead overlaid on top
of each other). Both formats (the stack and the grid) enable the
comparison of small collections of images, the former privileging
the analytical engagement with the content, the latter offering a
more synthesized and illustrative output that is particularly apt
for presentation purposes.

The grid enables the comparison of (often small) collections
of ranked images. Images are arrayed in a grid from highest to
lowest (following their engagement values, or ranking in the case
of search engine results), with columns representing different
spaces (e.g., hashtags, platforms, time frames, or languages).
The grid gathers images in the same optical space and provides
the structure to appreciate 'continuities and resonances' (Ahmed,
2017) across them. In this regard, the grid is a synoptic format
as it allows (following the term's etymology) viewing together
a group of elements in a structured way. The format has been
used over the years for various goals, including statistical visual
analysis, following the principle of small multiples (Tufte, 2001),

where one puts a series of charts side by side to allow fast visual comparison. When used to compare networked images and their rankings, the grid is characterized by an ordering axis (Engelhardt et al., 2016) where images' spatial organization (but not their exact position) is meaningful. This feature makes the grid a ranked space (as opposed to the metric space of a scatter plot), and it is particularly apt for comparing engagement across platforms with very different metrics (e.g., Instagram likes, retweets, Google Images rankings) where sheer numbers are very different.

The grid is apt for analytical purposes, as one can closely read individual images, compare them with those in other columns, and evaluate their position (based on engagement). There are also other modes for comparing collections of ranked images that privilege the synthetic view. With image stacks, one assembles images on top of each other, retaining their ranking. Compared to the grid, the image stack offers a synthetic view of the images from each collection. When applied to the study of platform visual vernaculars (see figure 3.5), at a glance, image stacks offer a visual summary of the formats and styles by which a platform represents an issue. The traditional technique entails combining the top ten images into one new image, stacking them, and making them semi-transparent. The resulting image stack is a montage of multiple perspectives in one synthetic view, where similar structures (such as image macros) in the same image set are foregrounded. Another option is to assemble images computationally through software that selects fragments of the top ten images and combines them into one new image (see figure 3.7). In this case, the resulting stack will focus on the differences among the same image set and will foreground details (as opposed to overall structures).

The differences between the two ways to operationalize the image stacking technique exemplify how these visualization formats should not be perceived as neutral. Many technical decisions made throughout the visualization process influence the final result, affecting what is emphasized and what is pushed to the background. It is essential to consider how each display format (and the technical steps and tools used to design them) influences the type of analysis one can make. Affirming that visual models embed specific forms of knowledge (Drucker, 2014), each

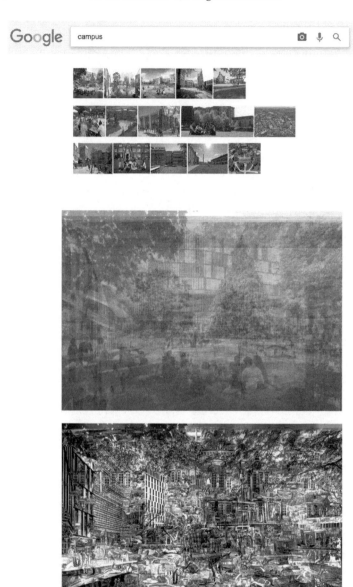

3.7 What does a campus look like? Image stacks for the same collection of images (top) obtained by querying [campus] on Google Image Search. The same collection is visualized as a layered image (centre) and as an assemblage (bottom). Visualizations by Federica Bardelli. Google Image Search thinks a campus is mostly students sitting together on a lawn.

display format may support distinct analytical procedures (while foreclosing others). For example, grids attempt to overcome the limitations of browsing a folder of images by enabling a vertical and horizontal reading of ranked images per platform. In contrast, image stacks allow for fast detection of differences and similarities between multiple image sets, offering a synthetic overview of the visual features of each collection (such as orientation, style, and content).

Finally, it is important to realize that these visualizations are a way into further research, not a way out of it. To make sense of the visualizations, one needs to do a close reading of the images that have been layered (or displayed as a grid) and of the users that posted them, taking into account the meaning that has been assigned to them on the platform (e.g., by way of captions and hashtags). There are also considerations to be made about what is missing from an image grid or stack. Apart from using these visualizations to explore the content of a collection of images, an active research attitude may also involve paying attention to what is not included in the visualization. Who or what is missing from a platform's depiction of a particular issue? Attending to what is missing from a folder of images is at the centre of the next chapter, which focuses on techniques for studying bias in the visual representation of various issues online.

Further Readings

- Marres, N. (2015). Why map issues? On controversy analysis as a digital method. *Science, Technology, & Human Values*, 40(5), 655–86. https://doi.org/10.1177/0162243915574602.
- Niederer, S. (2019). *Networked Content Analysis: The Case of Climate Change*. Amsterdam: Institute of Network Cultures.
- Pearce, W., Özkula, S. M., Greene, A. K., Teeling, L., Bansard, J. S., Omena, J. J. & Rabello, E. T. (2020). Visual cross-platform analysis: digital methods to research social media images. *Information, Communication & Society*, 23(2), 161–80. https://doi.org/10.1080/1369118X.2018.1486871.

4

Critical Images: Exposing Inequalities with Visual Research

This chapter reviews key literature on algorithmic bias and inequalities in (visual) data sets. It also introduces techniques for studying image bias and demonstrates (visual) research methods for studying how and why specific images spread more than others. The chapter ends with strategies for public-facing presentations of research outcomes.

Introduction[6]

A large news photograph of a migrant boat packed with people is overlaid with a heat map visualizing the aggregated results of eye-tracking research. The heat map visualizes the distribution of attention by showing bright red zones where the test persons have looked the most; green and yellow show those areas where the eyes have travelled only briefly. Other parts of the image remained entirely unseen by the test persons, and they are now clearly visible. Next to the large photograph hangs a display that looks like a contact sheet, a grid of small-sized news photographs that have been meticulously annotated to indicate compositional lines and fixation points, pinpointing the particular parts of the image that received the most views.

This installation, titled *Gazeplots* (figure 4.1), is by the Dutch artist Coralie Vogelaar as part of a larger series of artworks addressing the spread of news imagery. In this series, Vogelaar asks why certain news images are featured time and time again while others simply 'vanish into oblivion' (FOMU, 2017). Her work demonstrates digital visual research in various ways, including the study of images, the experimentation with digital technologies (in this particular case, the use of eye-tracking software), and the annotation and visualization of her research materials for further research and discussion. The urgency of Vogelaar's work is heightened by her choice of subject. Namely, affective images of refugees and protests are overlaid with 'dry' software output. They are hard to watch and make us question the place and status digital technologies have in our daily lives and the decisions we make on the basis of their outputs.

Such critical visual work can inform broader questions, also regarding more recent technologies including AI and machine learning. This chapter explores research from art and academia that formulates and responds to questions concerning algorithmic inequalities, by exposing or analysing injustices through visual research. First, we explore the topic of inequality in data sets and discuss research on algorithmic bias. Second, we illustrate techniques for studying image bias with our own research on the representation of pregnancy in search engine results. Third, we look further into questions of representation in day-to-day images, in stock photography and social media images, and how to study which images spread *better* than others online. We conclude by discussing how critical images travel outside of the research setting, making it into the gallery and the courtroom and reaching a wider public.

While this chapter has a particular thematic focus (studying algorithmic visual bias), the projects we illustrate employ some analytical techniques discussed in more detail in other chapters. The research presented in this chapter makes use of visual digital research practices that involve building a collection of images (see chapter 1), displaying the images in different spatial arrangements (see chapter 2), close-reading smaller sets of 'top' (as in, most engaging) images, and comparing visual vernaculars across queries (see chapter 3)

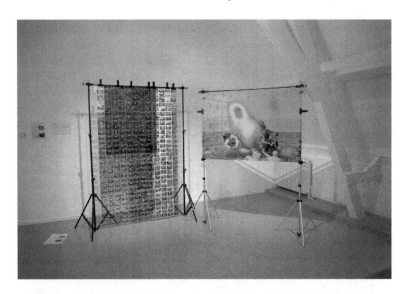

4.1 The installation *Gazeplots* by Coralie Vogelaar (2017), as presented at the Impakt Festival in 2018.

Algorithm bias

The pervasive spread of artificial intelligence has given rise to a body of critical work[7] on the bias and inequalities in the algorithms and training data sets used in artificial intelligence technologies. This work contributes to debunking the myth of artificial intelligence as a *neutral technology*. As writer and artist James Bridle (2018) put it, these new technologies are often thought of as having the potential to level out societal differences and allow for more equitable decision-making. In reality, machine learning systems do not live in a vacuum. They learn from existing data sets, are trained to decide what it is they are seeing, and they need to be given a frame of reference to make an interpretation of what is shown. Therefore, even though machine learning algorithms may be designed to be impartial, it has been widely demonstrated and explored that existing biases and inequalities creep into artificial intelligence (O'Neil, 2016; Chou et al., 2017; Sinders, 2017; Vincent, 2018; Lambrecht & Tucker, 2020). This may already happen on the level of the training data set.

Machine learning technologies rely heavily on the quality and representativeness of the data sets used to train them, and research has found that training and benchmarking practices are 'heavily concentrated on datasets originating from a small number of well-resourced institutions across the field as a whole' (Koch et al., 2021). The use of a training set that is too limited, too small, and has too little diversity is likely to result in an algorithm that takes on and amplifies such a bias. Another possible source of bias concerns who has compiled and trained the data. If the data set is curated by, or the algorithm is trained by, a team that lacks diversity in gender, race, ability, and other factors, it is likely that the algorithm takes on and perpetuates, if not amplifies, such a bias (Chou et al., 2017; Sinders, 2017). The urgency of taking on such issues through critical research cannot be denied, as these technologies are increasingly being implemented in many areas of life and society.[8]

But bias and lack of representation are not just arising from limited and biased training sets, or the professionals working on compiling and training with them. To further complicate matters, algorithms like those used in Google Image Search continue learning through their use (e.g., what users query and which search results they click on) (Bogers et al., 2020). Each time we share, use, or engage with an image online, we – the users – are 'feeding an array of immensely powerful artificial intelligence systems information about how to identify people and how to recognise places and objects, habits and preferences, race, and gender identifications, economic statuses, and much more' (Paglen, 2016). How visual digital research may probe such bias can be illustrated by the work of scholar Safiya Umoja Noble. She has probed Google Image Search to demonstrate the racial bias produced by the engine and its users, by querying for 'professional' and 'unprofessional hairstyles for work' (2018), and found how mostly Caucasian hair was shown as 'professional' and black hair almost entirely depicted under 'unprofessional hair' (Noble, 2018; Bogers et al., 2020), as can be seen in figure 4.2.

The image results for 'professional' and 'unprofessional hairstyles for work' do not represent the first time the search engine demonstrated bias. Google had already made headlines a few years earlier when a black man and woman were automatically labelled as 'gorillas' by its Photos service. Google's response was to deactivate image categories such as *gorilla* and *chimpanzee* altogether to avoid offensive miscategorizations in the future (Vincent, 2018). Such mismatches demonstrate that machines can have a bias – whether built-in or learnt along the

4.2 Image search results for 'professional hair for work' (left) and 'unprofessional hair for work' (right) on Google Image Search.

way – that can have real discriminatory consequences. These consequences become more severe when algorithms are linked to automated control processes, such as self-driving cars, or act as primary 'consultants' in decision-making processes.[9]

While this chapter focuses on visual research, it is important to note that algorithmic bias occurs in text too. There are famous examples from search engine results in Google Web Search. On the cover of her book, Safyija Umoja Noble depicts how, for the partial query 'Why are black women so', Google autocompletes it with phrases like 'Why are black women so angry', 'Why are black women so loud', 'Why are black women so mean' (Noble, 2018). Other examples have laid bare gender-biased results. Figure 4.3 depicts an experiment to test the bias in Google Translate. The researcher took gendered sentences in English, e.g., *she is the president*, *he is a nurse*, and translated them into Turkish and back to English. As the Turkish language does not have gendered pronouns, these were lost when translating the English text to Turkish:

> Translating back to English required the AI-based translation algorithm to analyse and associate a gender with the type of role being described. The data that is used to teach the AI has strong

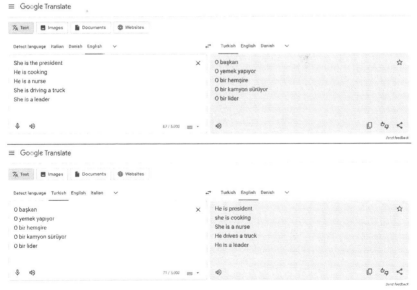

4.3 Probing gender bias in the Google translation algorithm (Bano, 2018; recreated by the authors).

gender stereotypes. The AI therefore decided it must be HE who is president, driving a truck or a leader, and it must be a SHE who is cooking and is a nurse. (Bano, 2018)

Alongside strategies for auditing algorithmic systems (Sandvig et al., 2014; Rogers, 2021), researchers and artists alike have also formulated responses to bias in the data – for instance, by outlining design and research principles for fair, understandable, or feminist AI and data practices,[10] or by actively filling the gaps in the data set.

An example of the latter is the audiovisual project 'Salvaging birds' by Maya Livio. The project takes to the realm of bird conservation, reliant on data as any conservation effort is these days, and finds biases and misclassifications akin to that of human data sets. In the project, Livio found a male bias in bird conservation data sets, both in terms of the bird specimens kept in the natural history archive and audio archives of birdsong recordings. As a response, Livio put birdsongs from the archive through an audio-generation neural net to produce 'more sonic material to fill in these gaps of the datasets' (D'Ignazio et al., 2021). The project is an example of how one can employ visual research methods and work with generative AI to critically and actively counter the lack of diversity in a data set.

In the following sections, we will discuss more examples of the study of algorithmic bias in the visual representation of various issues online. First, we look at ways to study how search engine results are affected by (visual) bias, with an analysis of the representation of pregnancy on Google Image Search. Second, we move to strategies to study inequalities and bias in the circulation of images online. Here, we look at successful and unsuccessful images, paying attention to how user practices (such as liking, commenting, and reposting) may lead to uneven visibility of certain images over others. Lastly, we point out how the outcomes of such critical research may have a life outside of academia, and be presented in galleries and even courtrooms.

Studying image bias: the case of pregnancy online

The study we would like to introduce here is very similar in spirit to the example of Safiya Umoja Noble and her queries for (un)professional hair. In Noble's work on algorithmic oppression through search engines, she describes close readings of 'open-ended racial and gendered search' queries (Noble, 2018, p. 44) to articulate value systems and biases reflected in their results. By studying search results through an intersectional lens, you can analyse search results to highlight social stratification along the lines of race and gender, but also how they intersect with, for example, sexual orientation and ability. This approach is informed by the long history of feminist critiques on the representation of women, which also extends to the representation of pregnant women.[11]

In a study exploring platform-specific bias in the contemporary algorithmic media landscape, we conducted a comparative analysis of the representation of pregnancy on the web and social media (Bogers et al., 2020). In the study, we use the method of cross-platform image analysis (which is presented in detail in chapter 3). Following platforms' specific properties (such as most upvoted on Reddit and most liked on Instagram), we collected the most engaged-with images for the query [pregnant OR pregnancy]. The collected images are then analysed with two visualization techniques: the image grid (with the twenty most engaged-with images in a comparative overview) and the stack, which combines only the top ten most engaged-with pictures layered into a single image.[12]

The analysis demonstrates how online visual materials, such as social media content related to pregnancy, showed bias and a lack of diversity. While platform-specific perspectives range from lists of pregnancy tips on Pinterest to pregnancy information and social support systems on Twitter and pregnancy humour on Reddit, each platform presents a predominantly white, able-bodied, and heteronormative perspective on pregnancy (Bogers et al., 2020).

To address which particular visual representations of pregnancy were foregrounded while making others invisible, we added a small experiment to the research, formulated a *counter-query* for the term 'pregnancy', and compared the results for two queries – [pregnant OR pregnancy] and [unwanted pregnancy] – in Google Image Search (images.google.com) in English. The collected images were then analysed for the absence or presence of specific visual markers, such as the presence of the *baby* in the picture (belly, baby, sonogram, or medical image), the presence of a *pregnant woman* in the picture (including her face), the presence of *other people* in the image (partners, people who appear to be the parents or friends of the pregnant woman), and *ethnic diversity* (do we see only white people or also people of colour?). These markers act as proxies for being able to say something about the way the pregnant woman is positioned in the English search results of the dominant search engine Google.com.

A pregnant belly without a face can be seen to reduce the pregnant woman to a disembodied (or even a medicalized) vessel that is void of a further human context. The focus on the baby *inside* the womb (either visible or represented through the pregnant belly) can be seen to draw the attention away from the woman and towards the baby. The presence of other people in the image depicts the pregnant woman in a *relational* manner; she is not isolated but, rather, connected to others. Her pregnancy is explicitly linked to her relationships and how these might be affected positively or negatively by the pregnancy. Taking into account the presence/absence of white people and people of colour in relation to these markers could tell us how the representation of pregnancy might be racialized.

Comparing [pregnancy] and [unwanted pregnancy] results shows a remarkably distinct visual representation, especially when looking at a larger number of search results. But even when looking at only the first top ten images in Google Image Search (using images.google.com), the [pregnancy] images foreground the unborn baby in the belly (see figure 4.4). The images of the pregnant women are cropped to depict only the pregnant belly, sometimes with hands. The backgrounds are neutral, and the settings show little social context. The query [unwanted pregnancy] presents more diverse imagery, where women are presented in full, and their distressed male partners (often in or on a bed) and supportive friends make an appearance. The settings are less neutral, and we see the interiors of houses and what appears to be a high school restroom. The protagonist of this visual space is not the baby, as we saw in the pregnancy imagery, but rather the pregnancy test or abortion pills. Men are predominantly shown as either the sexual partner in bed or as distant (physical distance, looking away, or not present because they are sleeping), whereas other people, such as friends and medical staff, are shown as empathic, putting an

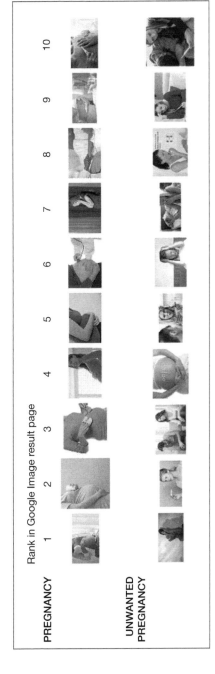

4.4 Overview of the top ten Google Image Search results for [pregnant OR pregnancy] (top rows), and the top ten images for [unwanted pregnancy] (bottom row). Source: Bogers et al. (2020).

arm or hand on a shoulder around the woman, looking in the same direction as or directly at the pregnant person. Empathy is shown to come from friends, much less from male partners, who are now there, but more often than not presented as withdrawn.[13] In general, these images can be said to tell a story of gendered role patterns and expectations around sex, reproduction, and family making.

Comparing the presence/absence of people of colour across the query and counter-query, white people are foregrounded more in the first. However, people of colour are significantly more visible when looking beyond the first twenty Google Image results for [unwanted pregnancy]. Although not as striking as Noble's query for unprofessional hairstyles, these are noticeable differences, and such patterns perpetuate negative connotations that feed into damaging stereotypes. By the same token, we might say in this case that whiteness dominates the more neutral query while people of colour are marginalized in this representational realm. While this is only a small experiment, it calls for a follow-up study that looks beyond the top results and again asks: *where* (and how far from the top) and when diversity is resonating in search engine results about (unwanted) pregnancy, what exactly is diversified, and how.

Successful visuals: stock photography spreading across platforms

For researchers of visual cultures online, another interesting object of study in the realm of visual representation is stock photography, which is also used in abundance in pregnancy-related content and is not ideology-free – nor is it very diverse. Giorgia Aiello argues that stock photographs are telling of how society sees itself, play a central role in visual culture, and are essential to the way people engage with media content (2016). For example, her research on stock photography demonstrates changing ideas of gender and how best-selling stock imagery of women has changed from 'sex object to gritty woman' (Miller, 2017). Aiello argues that these 'generic images', the large players such as Getty Images that create and host them, and how they spread globally may shape specific hegemonic 'ways of seeing' (Aiello, 2016; Aiello & Woodhouse, 2016).

Shoreditch Office	(33 images)	(1414 TIMES)	woman
Corporate			female
Modern Office Shoot			Portrait
portrait of young woman on plain background			office
Head and shoulders portrait			Young
woman running at nighttime			businesswoman
Female maker doing hand work in garage workshop.			girl
Surfer friends			Smiling
Urban Portrait			working
Family lifestyle			Tablet

4.5 Top ten most used words in the titles of the photos of the Getty Images Lean In Collection (right) and top ten most used full titles for the photos (left).

In a study with the Digital Methods Initiative, Aiello et al. (2016) looked into the feminist politics of stock photography across representation, circulation and re-contextualization by way of the Getty Images Lean In Collection, a special image collection 'devoted to the powerful depiction of women, girls and families' (LeanIn.org). To characterize the set, researchers looked at the images themselves and analysed their descriptions in the database (figure 4.5). Based on the words that occurred the most in the image descriptions and titles, they concluded that a typical image in this 'empowerment' collection would show a young woman in an office, smiling and possibly holding a tablet (Aiello et al., 2016). Zooming in further on women's representation in the Lean In Collection, the combinations that are most likely to be found are images of white women with brown hair who are 24–29 years old (with Caucasian women being by far the most represented in the set). Images portraying women in tech – specifically created to promote more diversity in stock imagery – are, in fact, hardly used in contexts of tech journalism, and images with women of colour were generally only used in the context of web content 'focused on black communities, immigrants or Muslims' (Aiello et al., 2016).

Even explicit attempts to portray more diversity in stock photography, such as the Lean In Collection, but also the 'Genderblend' project (a visual trend promoted by Getty Images aimed at portraying gender identities in a more inclusive and diverse way), struggle to overcome the imbalance of who is depicted (and who is not) as members of society (Aiello & Woodhouse, 2016, p. 367). In their research, Aiello and Woodhouse address the '"politics" of stock photography' by asking how 'Genderblend recontextualize[s] issues related to gender inequality in the light of Getty's corporate interests.' In their analysis of the dedicated collection of gender diversity, they find the company's photo collection emphasizes 'people's individual abilities (e.g. nurturing, leadership, fitness), relationships (e.g. with a child, with co-workers), and occupations (e.g. father, engineer, soldier)' (2016, p. 11). Furthermore, they find that the Genderblend collection 'works to reinscribe its "trailblazing" imagery into easily grasped clichés and assumptions'. The importance of such critical work lies in the widespread use of stock photography in commercial spaces of advertising, marketing, and even news journalism, and how it thus has taken up an important role in representing 'society'.

Studying the uneven visibility of social media images

Other researchers have turned their attention to the successful spread of other kinds of online images, namely those produced by 'organic' users (i.e., 'regular' users of social media). For example, media scholar Marloes Geboers (2019) has studied the resonance of war and conflict imagery on social media platforms. In her study of the engagement with images of Alan Kurdi, the young boy who washed ashore on the coast of the Mediterranean Sea and became a heart-wrenching symbol of the refugee crisis, Geboers found that many users visually engage with images of distant suffering.

Figure 4.6 depicts the top five images shared per day on Instagram after Alan Kurdi drowned on 2 September 2015 in the Mediterranean Sea. Images are ranked from most to least liked in each column, and coloured rectangles display their relative engagement. The grid, read from left to right, shows how rapidly user-created modified versions (often illustrations) 'take over from the original photographs' (Geboers, 2019, p. 12). Following the colour coding, the visualization also shows how volatile the success of certain images is, as, after heightened user activity on the day after the death of the boy, engagement quickly dwindles down.

In sharing 'reworked images' (for instance, collages that depict the boy peacefully sleeping in his bed), these affective publics 'write oneself into [this] tragedy' and unwillingly turn the

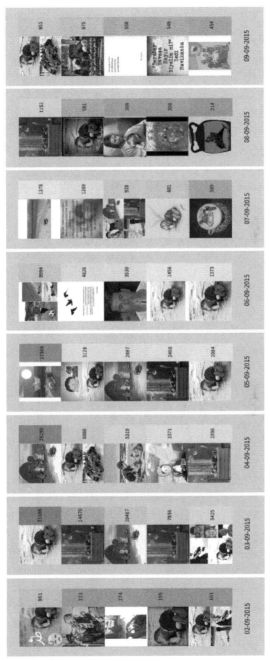

4.6 Top five most liked images per day (2 to 9 September 2015) on Instagram with the hashtags #aylan, #kiyiyavuraninsanlik and #humanitywashedashore.

attention to themselves and their emotions rather than the issue and its victims. The analysis shows how the images created to engage with the tragedy crowd out the images about the tragedy itself, turning the attention towards the emotions of those empathizing with the issue rather than the issue itself.

Critical visual research in different contexts

Critical images may travel across different contexts, moving away from the academic context in which they were originally designed. Figure 4.7 shows the previously discussed study of Alan Kurdi as presented by Marloes Geboers for a television documentary. Rather than guiding the viewers through the visualization as one may do during an academic presentation or a class, the visualization here has become a backdrop for story-telling. The ranked lists of images, sorted by level of engagement and organized per day, have become a decor that signifies that the affective responses to this dramatic event have become a research object that can be explored and understood.

Of course, there are plenty of examples of visual research that is conducted outside of (or in collaboration with) academic

4.7 Media scholar Marloes Geboers, surrounded by the visualization by Gabriele Colombo, discusses the study for a documentary, 'Kitten or Refugee?', by Tina Farifteh, broadcast by Dutch public broadcaster VPRO.

contexts, be it in art, journalism, or elsewhere. Forensic Architecture (figure 4.8) is a collective of architects, investigative journalists, artists, and filmmakers at Goldsmiths University in London that deploys the language and tools of architecture combined with open-source intelligence to collect, organize, and present 'spatial evidence in the context of armed conflict and political struggles' (e-flux, 2017).

Considering such independent and engaged design to be 'not a profession but an attitude', as put forward by László Moholy-Nagy in his book *Vision in Motion* (1947), design scholar Alice Rawsthorn describes Forensic Architecture as 'attitudinal designers wrestling with ... urgent challenges', who '[take] on extreme situations' (2022, p. 13), from the fire that destroyed Moria refugee camp in 2020, to police brutality during Black Lives Matter protests (2020 and onwards). The work of Forensic Architecture and others has been referred to with the term 'investigative aesthetics' (Fuller & Weizman, 2021), where the sensibilities frequently associated with art, architecture, and other similar practices are put to use in activist practices. The melding of different sensibilities results in poignant research outputs that have the power to travel across settings and reach a broader and more heterogeneous audience. We mention them here as a powerful example of transdisciplinary and participatory visual digital research with societal impact.

4.8 Forensic Architecture (2015), multiple images and reconstructed bomb clouds are arranged within a 3D model of Rafah, Gaza.

Conclusion

The importance of critical visual research cannot be overstated. By misrepresenting or oversimplifying complex issues through biased visuals, we risk perpetuating stereotypes, and misconceptions, and even exacerbating societal injustices. Hence, the research into visual bias is not just an academic endeavour but a societal imperative, to ensure fairness and equity in the age of information.

Emphasizing our commitment to studying visual materials using visual methodologies, we believe that to understand these materials authentically, one must stay immersed in their visual context while also taking into account the textual lives of these visual materials (e.g., textual queries, metadata, image captions). The research methods we highlight throughout this chapter (and, indeed, the entirety of this book) emphasize the centrality of visual formats. In chapter 2, we delved into visualizations of extensive image collections, asserting that these visualizations serve as a tool that allows researchers to shift from broad overviews to detailed insights. Chapter 3 turned to the examination of visual arrangements for smaller image collections, spotlighting structures such as the grid and stack. Furthermore, this chapter underscored the potential of image displays for facilitating comparative analysis of smaller image collections or crafting compelling narratives beyond scholarly contexts.

In the following chapter, we will delve deeper into the application of these visual formats in participatory contexts. While this chapter elucidated techniques to identify and highlight biases and omissions in data, the next chapter will similarly shine a spotlight on absent elements within image collections and discuss how participatory methods can bridge these gaps. Taking cues from contemporary data feminism theories, which challenge researchers to recognize and address societal inequalities magnified by data-driven technologies, we introduce visual tactics for collaborative endeavours. In our discussion, we contemplate the roles visual tools can assume in facilitating public participation, illustrating research environments where participants are encouraged to interact and respond to the presented data. These participatory research practices work on a continuum where some visual tools primarily serve the researcher, while others are crafted to democratize interpretation, fostering participation and joint reflection.

Further Readings

- Bucher, T. (2018). *If ... Then: Algorithmic Power and Politics*. Oxford University Press. https://doi.org/10.1093/oso/9780190493028.001.0001.
- Fuller, M. & Weizman, E. (2021). *Investigative Aesthetics: Conflicts and Commons in the Politics of Truth*. London, New York: Verso.
- Noble, S. U. (2018). *Algorithms of Oppression: How Search Engines Reinforce Racism*. New York University Press.

5

Participatory Images:
Talking Back to Maps

This chapter starts by introducing (data) feminist theory to develop critical ways to study online images. It then demonstrates visual methods for participatory practices that involve different publics throughout the research process. The chapter ends with reflections on the role of visualizations in designing participation for digital research.

Introduction

A group of people stand in front of a large board containing a printed map of the city of Copenhagen (figure 5.1). They interact with the map and discuss among themselves: they choose pictures from a deck of cards and co-write photo captions before placing them onto the map using pins and pieces of string. The pictures they are placing around the map were taken during an earlier activity, when members of different marginalized communities were asked to visually document their experiences in urban space, capturing situations that negatively or positively affect their sense of belonging to the city. During the workshops, participants from these different communities select the pictures they would like to discuss, jointly annotate the images, and position them on the map to indicate where they were taken. Together, they create links between photographic depictions of the city, their personal experiences and views, and a cartographic representation of the urban space. The participants work with digitally captured images (in this instance, using a custom mobile app), and subsequently printed onto paper. The figure represents a situation where visual digital research becomes participatory, the boundaries between researchers and subjects are blurred, and communities are invited to talk back to (or even co-design) maps and visualizations that foreground their experiences and personal views.[14]

In this chapter, we introduce participatory methods in visual digital research. We first review literature that invites reflexivity on the role of the researcher and emphasizes how observations about the impacts of the research contribute to and shape the research process itself. Reflecting on the effect of the research on the actors involved is particularly important in projects that include public participatory work when people are actively invited to talk back to the map or contribute to the research in other ways. Second, we explore the roots of recent (data) feminist theory to learn how a practice of care (Calvillo González & Mesa del Castillo, 2018) may be integrated into design, digital, and participatory research. Third, we discuss recent research projects situated in Science and Technology Studies (STS) and intersectional feminism, drawing in different ways of knowing (both from the researchers themselves, their objects of study, and public participation) and considering matters of concern (Latour, 2005). Fourth, we explore what happens to these research strategies when taken to the digital, which concerns remain stable and which new challenges arise.

We close the chapter by presenting visual formats for participatory work that combine online and offline research developed in projects in Paris, Rijeka, and Copenhagen. These research projects illustrate how talking back to images offers a productive space for joint reflections on matters of concern. Such an invitation to 'talk back to images', from geographical maps to data visualizations, illustrates how we approach and understand participation in our own projects. By participation, we mean a range of practices that invite those who are the object of study to take part in the entire analytical process, offering perspectives,

5.1 Workshop of participatory map-making from the 'Urban Belonging' project.

interpretations, and insights that make the study better informed, more situated, and more inclusive.

Knowledge in the making

When thinking about the different kinds of knowledge in the making during research, we can also think about how we – as researchers – can capture these various layers of inquiry. In *Reassembling the Social*, Bruno Latour proposes that researchers need four notebooks: one for logging the 'enquiry itself', a second for structured note-taking (e.g., organized by chronology or category), a third for 'ad libitum writing' of ideas that pop up when preparing and conducting the research, and a fourth to 'register the effect of the written account on the actors whose world has been either deployed or unified' (Latour, 2005, pp. 134–5). With this proposal of the distinct notebooks, Latour separates different types of information, insights, and reflexivity. The first notebook documents the research process while also inviting reflexivity on what transformations the research and the researcher undergo throughout the journey. Another way to capture this information would be to create and annotate a research protocol diagram (Niederer & Colombo, 2019). The second is what can be considered the data set: the well-organized and cleaned-up research input that is ready to be processed and analysed further. The third notebook is for preliminary note-taking and capturing ideas and associations, while studying in preparation for and while doing the research. The fourth captures the effect of the research on the actors involved. This step is often forgotten but is especially important in projects that include public participatory work, when people are actively invited to talk back to the map or contribute to the research in other ways. What does the participatory practice do to and for its participants? With the four notebooks, Latour encourages the researcher to log the process of knowledge in the making. This creative and analytical process can be entangled with traditions, mechanisms, and conventions.

Latour proposes thinking of 'exposing how things are assembled, constructed, not as a way to dismantle them' (Puig de la Bellacasa, 2017, p. 39). Nor is a focus on the dynamics of knowledge *in the making* a way to become suspicious of the mechanisms underpinning their construction (like a conspiracy theorist would). Instead, focusing on matters of concern can 'emancipate a public' from seemingly objectified matters of fact. Furthermore, such a focus recognizes the researcher (or the critic, as described in his piece 'Why has critique run out of steam?') as the one who assembles and 'offers the participants arenas in which to gather' (Latour, 2007, p. 246). Importantly, Latour stresses that researchers should realize that 'if something is constructed, then it means it is fragile and thus in great need of care and caution' (p. 246).

Matters of care

Recognizing the need for care and caution in research, Maria Puig de la Bellacasa proposes to include 'matters of care' in the study and 'articulation of ethically and politically demanding issues' (Puig de la Bellacasa, 2011, p. 94; Calvillo González & Mesa del Castillo, 2018). In her work, she draws on Latour, Stengers, and Haraway, combining attention to the 'lives of things' and how 'respect for the concerns embodied in the things we represent implies attention to the effects of our accounts on the life of things' (p. 39). Maria Puig de la Bellacasa stresses that even when we are critical of critique and how it is usually voiced, in reference to Latour, we still need research approaches that unveil underlying power structures and oppression in the assembly or gathering of things, beyond the reflexivity of the individual researcher alone. Thus she proposes 'matters of care', stressing the importance of protection and care when working on matters of concern. Puig de la Bellacasa, therefore, calls for attention to concerns as a *practice of care* and 'as something we can *do* as thinkers and knowledge creators' (p. 41). She thus does not turn away from the approach to matters of concern but wants to layer and extend it to add the dimension of care in 'more than human worlds, remaining responsive to material obligations while eschewing moralism and reductive humanist explanations' (p. 41).

The proposed practice of doing research with care has been operationalized in the fields of design and architecture by Calvillo González and Mesa del Castillo (2018). Their operationalization of matters of care into five pointers for 'designing with care' to include in their design educational practice could also be considered helpful starting points for a participatory research setting. In their approach, they reconsider the built environment as 'tender infrastructures', both in need of and offering care, and the city as an 'accumulation of socio-material pieces constituted by heterogeneous networks of humans, artefacts, practices, non-humans and spaces' (Farías & Bender, 2010, p. 179). For the repositioning of materiality, they find the work by Noortje Marres particularly valuable, as she demonstrates (through her work on smart meters and other examples of *material partici-pation*) (Marres, 2015a) that 'the policy of these technologies does not reside in themselves, but rather in the form in which they are used in different situations and contexts and, above all, in their capacity to redistribute agencies' (Calvillo González & Mesa del Castillo, p. 179).

These repositionings, built on feminist and STS scholarship, laid the groundwork for an innovative educational approach that starts from inviting students, in the vein of Puig de la Bellacasa (2011), to 'assemble things that have been neglected'. This approach leads to questions such as 'For whom do you design? Who is the centre of interest in what in architecture is usually called "program"?' Similarly, in the choice of materials, the students are invited to think of materials that are often neglected. Most importantly, the students are stimulated to put underrepresented agents at the core of their architectural design, those who 'hav[e] been forgotten until recently by architecture: the environment (Banham, 1969), climate (Scuderi, 2014), plants, animals, et cetera, which can only be thought of as part of a continuum between nature and culture, where all entities are taken into account simultaneously' (Puig de la Bellacasa, 2011, p. 184). Calvillo González and Mesa del Castillo (2018) also express the need to understand the importance of locality. A situated design approach takes seriously the local stakeholders that are included, and thus affected, by the issues and objects under study, as will be discussed in the exemplary projects at the end of this chapter.

The tender infrastructures approach resonates strongly with design justice (as formulated by Sasha Costanza-Chock, 2020) and the principles of data feminism of Catherine D'Ignazio and Lauren Klein (2020). For instance, Gonzales and del Castillo describe the importance of identifying 'power imbalances articulated from and with the material' (2018, p. 179). In the practice of visualization, this connects to D'Ignazio and Klein's proposal for the development of 'feminist data visualisation', which entails a rethinking of binaries, a consideration of context and the making visible of labour (2016). The critical work from STS and feminist theory has similarly influenced digital and participatory research, as discussed in the following sections.

Data feminism

In digital research, too, scholars choose to include intersectional feminist concepts in their work. An influential example is the data feminism project and book by Catherine D'Ignazio and Lauren Klein, which critically addresses power imbalances in data science. Data feminism builds on intersectional feminist concepts such as the matrix of domination, developed by sociologist Patricia Hill Collins to capture the complex entanglement of privileges, leading to 'interlocking systems of oppression' based on race, class, and gender (Collins, 1990, p. 541). Data feminism ranges from examining and challenging power structures in data collection to embracing pluralism beyond binaries and hierarchies (D'Ignazio et al., 2021). A similar direction is put forward with Sasha Costanza-Chock's approach of design justice, which aims to 'spur our imaginations about how to move beyond a system of technology design largely organised around the reproduction of the matrix of domination. In its place, we need to imagine how all aspects of design can be reorganised around human capabilities, collective liberation, and ecological sustainability' (Costanza-Chock, 2020, p. 73).

Another concept at the heart of data feminism and similar approaches is that of situated knowledge, or *knowledges* (in plural), as put forward by Donna Haraway in response to the scientific 'quest for "objectivity"' (1988, p. 575) and the 'policing' of what is knowledge (1988), also present in Latour's writings on the construction of facts. Haraway counters this with situated, feminist objectivity that is localized rather than generalized, and connected to communities rather than individuals. A third concept highlighted as key to the intersectional feminist roots of data feminism is that of 'emotional labour' by Arlie Hochschild (1983), which acknowledges that the professional role of the researcher – and that of a participant, for that matter – can entail emotional work – for example, when working on topics that can be trauma-informed (Pichon et al., 2022).

In data feminism, these feminist theories are crucial to improving or even reinventing data science, as it is regarded as burdened by underlying power imbalances exacerbated by data-driven technology. As D'Ignazio and Klein point out, focusing on these intersecting *sources of power* helps us to look for the root causes of this imbalance: 'It is not a surprise that our technology is racist and sexist. When you live in a white supremacist, heteropatriarchal society, you get white supremacist, heteropatriarchal data systems' (D'Ignazio et al., 2021, p. 4). The book emphasizes the importance of 'form[ing] a position that recognises that inescapability, that tries to think through the potential harms, and that tries to anticipate and hopefully redress the harms that might come about when these systems are deployed in the world. This can also mean not deploying a particular system if there is harm detected' (D'Ignazio et al., 2021, p. 5). As Latour intimated with his four notebooks approach, data feminism requires reflexivity, in which researchers are aware of their standpoints and limitations (D'Ignazio et al., 2021).

The data feminism book outlines seven principles, including examining and challenging power (referring to the matrix of domination and oppression), elevating emotion and embodiment (which resonates with Haraway's *situated knowledges*), and making labour visible (acknowledging the time and (emotional) labour invested throughout the process, by both researchers and participants, as discussed by Hochschild and Pinchon). Before moving on to discuss how such data feminist practices may take shape in participatory research, we want to see how the computational turn has affected thinking about participatory practices. Furthermore, we explore how digital research may lead to methodological reconsiderations, which take shape in the kinds of visualizations used in participatory research practices.

Digital and participatory social research and the role of (feminist) visualization

Digital and data-driven research have brought new challenges to the realm of social and participatory research. One important concern relates to introducing digital tools in the analytical process. Marres and Gerlitz (2016) point to a 'methodological uncanny' (p. 23) when it comes to digital social research, referring to the employment of tools for data collection and analysis, which are often borrowed from other fields, 'have the capacity to serve multiple purposes' (p. 26), and enact different 'political, for-profit and ethical agendas'. Marres and Gerlitz contrast the entanglement of actors, goals, and agendas embedded in tools for data analytics with the notion of 'interface methods', an analytical approach that considers this complexity as a 'productive site of empirical engagement with wider research contexts, practices and apparatuses' (p. 27). They call for experimentation and attentiveness to 'both the alignment and the misalignment of the analytical capacities' (p.42) of the method, the data, user practices, and other research components. The recognition of misalignments between the analytical goals of the researcher and those of the tools for data analysis points to the participatory aspects of digital research, even if not explicitly. When digital researchers use digital tools in the research process, they rely on 'complex and unstable assemblages that draw together a diversity of people, things and concepts' (Harvey et al., 2013, p. 294). Such 'unstable assemblages' include the mechanisms of the platforms from which data are collected, the users populating these platforms, and the technical aspects and rules specific to the device used.

The participatory aspect of digital research has been captured even more explicitly with the notion of 'redistribution of methods'. As Marres (2012) argued, digital technologies have made social research a 'distributed accomplishment', where online platforms, users, and researchers contribute to the practice of doing social research. In her view, digitization renders visible the distributed agencies of platforms, users, devices, and formats in co-producing knowledge when doing social research with the web. Instead of focusing on the debates regarding the novelty of digital methods, Marres draws attention towards how digital technologies have brought about a process of methodological distribution among different (human and non-human) actors involved in social research. Marres argues that, therefore, discussions about the digitization of social methods can be more productively framed as debates 'about participatory research methods' (2012). Considering digital research as a participatory activity means recognizing the contribution of different actors in the process of method-making and moving away from thinking about methods as 'proprietary' (Marres, 2012) to the researcher alone. Indeed, when doing research with the web, one is forced to recognize how such endeavour is necessarily affected by the actions of devices, data, users, and researchers, making its participatory nature visible.

An example would be online services such as Google Trends, which give insights into what users search for and show related terms based on those queries. Services such as Google Trends, whose data researchers might rely upon, are the result of a collaboration between users, digital platforms, and social researchers too. The notion of 'redistribution of methods' characterizes one way in which participation has entered the realm of digital social research, arguing how researchers, online users (albeit unintentionally), and digital platforms concur in producing data and knowledge.

The participatory turn in digital research can also be read as blurring the distinction between individuals and collectives. The digitization of social research enables researchers to bring individual stories back to the centre, no longer necessarily limiting themselves to analysing aggregate data. As Latour et al. (2012) argued, social sciences have always operated from a clear-cut distinction between studying elements and studying aggregates and attempted to determine how individual decisions related to collective actions. The digitization of social interactions has made it possible to follow individual items and their aggregation back and forth. Thus, such a 'two-level standpoint' can be replaced by a 'one-level standpoint', in which researchers can navigate 'datasets without making the distinction between the level of individual component and that of aggregated structure' (Latour et al., 2012). Encapsulated in the motto 'The whole is always smaller than its parts', this analytical shift is best illustrated by the visual analysis of networks of online profiles, allowing researchers to analyse individual actors and their connections simultaneously. The loss of distinction between individuals and aggregates, argued by Latour et al. (2012), resonates well with the invitation from data feminism to embrace plurality and multiplying perspectives in research. In their book, D'Ignazio and Klein (2020) invite researchers to listen to 'a multiplicity of voices, rather than one single loud or technical or magical one', to produce a 'more complete picture of the issue at hand' (2020, p. 136).

The work of multiplying perspectives in data-driven research, argued for by D'Ignazio and Klein (2020), again starts with the recognition of the researcher's own standpoint. From a feminist perspective, acknowledging the partiality of any point of view translates, first of all, into a demand for more reflexivity when doing research. This entails questioning the researcher's positionalities, but – given the distributed nature of digital research methods, as discussed above – also those of the tools involved in the research process. One research area where the call for more reflexivity has been taken up is visual network analysis. The need for reflexivity in the study and visualization of (issue) networks, a practice that has skyrocketed across scholarly fields, has been at the centre of methodological debates in the fields of critical data studies (Chun, 2018), and in social research, more broadly conceived (Venturini et al., 2014).

Resonating with the work of data feminism, new media scholar Wendy Chun argues that network science (including the algorithms underlying network visualization) is based on ideas of segregation, discrimination, and bias. Chun calls for a shift from the correlation of data to the study of co-relations, taking seriously that not all clusters are formed as homophilic echo chambers but that 'opposites attract' too (Chun, 2018). Chun, therefore, urges us to start questioning the axioms and assumptions underlying the basis of the algorithms, software, and interfaces we design, implement, and use. In their reflections on digital research and visualization practices, Venturini, Jacomy, and Pereira point to how much of the literature focuses on ways to create a network graph (which is a mathematical challenge more than anything else) and disregards how such an image should be read and conceptualized (2014). They define the work of interpreting network visualizations as characterized by vagueness and visual ambiguity, and invite researchers to embrace it as an 'asset for the analysis' (Venturini et al., 2014, p. 1). Venturini et al. stress the active research attitude that is required when working (and 'sometimes struggl[ing]') with network visualizations. When researchers produce and use such visualizations, they should challenge existing knowledge, search for new ways of knowing, and be open to unexpected findings (2014, p. 19). In the following section, we will discuss the production and use of visualizations for public participatory work, illustrated with examples from research projects in Paris, Rijeka, and Copenhagen.

Participatory images: opening up digital research to public participation with visualizations

From the recent development of tools for data visualization that enable researchers to visualize data to vernacular visualization practices and formats for public participation, visual methods play an important role in opening up the digital research process. The use of visualizations in (applied) research is not confined to those with training in information design. Many valuable tools today make it possible to create meaningful maps and diagrams for researchers without a design background. Digital research on platform content has led to visual innovations regarding tools and outputs. For instance, the tool RAWGraphs (Mauri et al., 2017) was explicitly designed to improve working with the outputs of digital methods tools, filling a gap and making data visualization accessible to a broader community of researchers, students, and (issue) professionals.

Historically, there are famous examples of innovative visualizations that come from outside the professional field of information design. Such work is referred to as 'vernacular visualizations', those that originate from 'outside the visualization community' and often violate some of the 'golden rules' of information design (Viégas & Wattenberg, 2008, p. 52). The tag cloud is a more recent example of this. The popular Wordle.net word cloud breaks many conventions (e.g., using random colours and directions without adding meaning) and yet, at the same time, provides a broader audience with a simple tool for creating an easily legible visualization of the most-used words in any body of text. The rise of vernacular visualizations, which might not follow data visualization tenets, has raised questions in the information design community about how data-driven visual artefacts might be evaluated. Non-expert visualizations may be evaluated not just against traditional parameters such as their efficiency in completing a task or retrieving information, but also concerning their power to sustain 'collaborative, communicative and coordinated' practices among the participants involved in a data-driven project (Snyder, 2017, p. 2109).

Relatedly, data feminist approaches to data visualization remind us how sometimes the goal of maps and other visualizations can have a high-level political purpose beyond their analytical power and, in doing so, can and should contravene the golden rules of the visualization of data (D'Ignazio et al., 2021). An example is geographical maps showing the overwhelming spread of particular phenomena (such as evictions or gender-based killings). In these maps, the pervasiveness of the phenomena visualized with a large number of geo-located pins makes it impossible to perform any spatial analysis. In these cases, the efficiency of the visualization as a tool for understanding geographical patterns is sacrificed for its rhetorical power: those looking at the map will be overwhelmed by it and puzzled about how ubiquitous the problem is (D'Ignazio et al., 2021). Maps of this type are very efficient in making a point, even if they do not align with data visualization's pursuit of efficiency and pattern recognition.

Displaying online images for collective speculation

In digital visual research, visual tools, specifically composite images (Colombo, 2018; Niederer & Colombo, 2019), can engage different publics in studying social issues. Here, composite images (resulting from combining multiple images into a new synthetical image) are collectively annotated in participatory sessions, where local stakeholders, experts, and decision-makers are confronted with the visualizations and asked to respond to them. 'NATURPRADI', the project introduced in chapter 2, was concerned with the online mapping of the issue of urban nature in the city of Paris (Ricci et al., 2017). To invite expert input, a series of composite images are designed and collectively interpreted during collaborative workshops. Composites, made of images posted on Twitter with particular keywords, such as 'nature', 'agriculture', or 'biodiversity', are meant to stimulate the observation of content-based clusters by displaying similar images close to each other (with the help of computer vision techniques). These composite images are then annotated during a workshop in a collective interpretation exercise (figure 5.2). In a process that can be described as 'graphical interpretation' (Drucker, 2010), workshop participants are asked to draw a visual layer summarizing their interpretation of the analysis on top of the composite image. As a final step, researchers may transform the interpretation layers in a diagram over the composite image.

In the 'NATURPRADI' project, the use of composite images (with a layer of interpretive annotations) allows for the engagement of different publics in the issue at hand by presenting them with the outcomes of analytical work and including them in the interpretation of those analytical outcomes, validating personal experiences and different perspectives. Indeed, each participant reacts to the composite differently: some highlight thematic clusters and label them, while others foreground individual images or add elements that appear absent from the composite. The invitation to talk back to the map allows participants to 'navigate the issue and imagine future public policies' (Ricci et al., 2017, p. 2) as each participant projects their concerns and interests onto the diagram. When asked to interpret the composite image, actors are prompted to confront

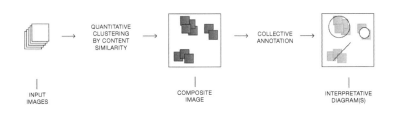

5.2 Process of the design of composite images and their collective interpretation in the 'NATURPRADI' project. Source: Niederer and Colombo (2019).

their perceptions with the online depiction of the issue under study: what *should* this map look like?

The space between what actors read into the map and what they think is missing opens up a process of collaborative speculation and, at times, agenda-setting. In addition, comparing multiple interpretations of the same composite image, summarized with the different interpretive diagrams produced by each actor during the workshop, provides ingredients for fruitful discussion among the workshop participants. In this example, visual formats (composite images and their diagrammatic interpretation) are used for participatory practices and the active construction of publics (DiSalvo, 2009) around the issue under study. They also activate a process of 'knowledge co-production' (Munk et al., 2019), or simply constitute 'conversation prompts' (Manzini, 2015) for the collective imagination of alternative versions of the issue under study.

Linking online images to personal stories: from data visualizations to visual artefacts for public participation

More recently, there have been other experiments with visual formats aimed at opening up online image research to public participation. With the term 'developing', Ricci et al. (2021) refer to a series of visual transformations (and outputs) that seek to move gradually from online images towards artefacts for public participation in the collaborative study of public issues. At the centre of this practice is the need to design visualization formats that, beyond their analytical power, can do more than map a particular issue, and allow for different publics to act upon it. In reaction to the critique that most digital research ends with an epiphanic moment of media reveal (Allen, 2020), summarized in a visualization, 'developing' seeks to design visual formats to enact a 'participatory and collective process of inquiry' (Ricci et al., 2021, p. 4). Narrated through the methodological steps of the 'DEPT' Project (figure 5.3), in which online images are used to initiate a collective reflection on urban politics and aesthetics (in the cities of Rijeka, Porto, and Paris), the 'developing register' aims at republishing networked visual materials into artefacts for participatory and collective inquiry. Moving back and forth across data visualization, algorithmic processing, editorial choices, and performative actions, the goal is to design visual formats that are not just for seeing and reading online images but are 'aimed at saying something with them ... and doing something through them' (Ricci et al., 2021, p. 9).

The process described in the 'DEPT' project is threefold, and each step produces a distinct visual format with its specific goal.

5.3 Annotated tableaux in Porto from the 'DEPT' project. Source: Ricci et al. (2021).

In the initial phase, researchers produce catalogues of images collected from various platforms (e.g., objects from Google Street View, visual elements extracted from Airbnb listings, tweets and associated images). Then, these catalogues are used in one-on-one dialogues with urban actors, who are guided through the materials and asked to comment, picking individual pictures and adding general observations. Personal notes, selected pictures, and annotation layers from each dialogue are then rearranged into tableaux, which are defined as structured compilations 'of images scraped and cropped, indexed by algorithms, annotated by hand, layered with the participants' personal narrative' (Ricci et al., 2021, p. 15). As such, these tableaux connect specific personal experiences to parts of the catalogues. In the final step of the process, which leans towards a performative action, tableaux are hung to the wall and read out loud by different participants, producing collective scores that foreground 'tensions and partial connections' among participants (Ricci et al., 2021, p. 17).

While the experiments described in the 'DEPT' project are tightly linked to the contexts and situations in which they took place, they still offer a rich and malleable vocabulary of techniques for those interested in using online images in collaborative settings; fixing image collections into data and media visualizations that reveal general patterns; expanding the visualizations into catalogues to be used as speculative prompts; conveying personal narratives into annotated tableaux; and then performing personal narratives through collective scores that assemble individual experiences. The formats, actions, and situations described constitute a valuable toolkit for developing digital (visual) traces into public voices – one sensitive to the networked nature of online images and that honestly engages with the traps of collective inquiry.

Working with participant-produced images: giving back the data

Visual formats and data visualizations (more specifically, catalogues of images and other materials) represent a valuable tool for opening up the data set to the participants in a study. As in the cases discussed above, visualizing and rearranging materials obtained from online data collection enable participants in a study to connect their personal experiences to the data. When participants are involved in the data collection process (as opposed to working with materials collected from the web), visual formats become even more critical for recognizing the work that goes into participating. In the book *The Participant*, Christopher M. Kelty (2019) traces the history of participation, arguing how its transformation into a rigid set of procedures has dwarfed its potential and how those taking part in it 'experience an attenuated, temporary feeling of personal contribution that ends almost as soon as it begins' (Kelty, 2019, p. 1). Among Kelty's recommendations on how to do participation is one about rendering the act of participating evident for those involved – 'make participation visible' – as, he argues, 'participation, at the very least, requires seeing oneself participate' (2019, p. 257). A similar concern, albeit not explicitly connected to participatory practices, is raised by D'Ignazio and Klein (2020). They argue how a feminist perspective on data-driven research should aim at making visible the labour of those involved in the data collection, analysis, and interpretation phases of the research process.

With inspiration from design justice principles of 'community-led design' (Costanza-Chock, 2020) and data feminist (D'Ignazio & Klein, 2020) principles of 'embracing pluralism', researchers from the Techno Anthropology Lab at Aalborg University Copenhagen and the Visual Methodologies Collective of the Amsterdam University of Applied Sciences designed a photovoice application, with the involvement of urban planning professionals as well as local marginalized communities (Madsen et al., 2023). In the 'Urban Belonging' project, also featured in the opening of this chapter, visual tools, maps, and data visualizations are used to engage participants from underrepresented groups in a collective activity of urban mapping. The project attempted to demonstrate how cities may work differently for various people, and explores 'how Copenhagen works as a space of belonging for marginalized communities' (Madsen et al., 2023, p. x). Experimenting with alternative ways to engage marginalized communities in the city of Copenhagen, the project involved participants who self-identified as deaf, LGBTQ+, homeless, ethnic minorities, people with physical disabilities, and people with mental vulnerabilities. Each participant was invited to document their lived experience of the city using participatory photography (photovoice) with a custom app that allows them to capture situations in the city and assess each photo and place according to their feeling of belonging. They were then invited to respond to the pictures taken by other participants within the app. In a series of in-person activities, participants collaborated to interpret their data, each bringing their catalogue of photos and places to discuss different perspectives on the city and find recurring themes.

Workshops in the 'Urban Belonging' project were organized around different data points produced by the participants, and used different visualization formats. First, each participant was given a deck of cards containing the photos they took with their annotations. Participants were then asked to select two images from the deck, place them on a collective map of Copenhagen and enrich the map with personal stories linked to each photo. Another activity focused on the routes taken by each participant: individual paths through the city were printed out, and the maps were used as conversation prompts to discuss 'how belonging is experienced on the move' (Madsen et al., 2023). Another map used as an elicitation device in the workshops visualized the reactions of participants to each other's photos, together with a card deck displaying the most contested photos (those causing the most diverse reactions), to initiate a conversation 'about aligned or conflicting feelings about the city' (Madsen et al., 2023). The results of the workshops are a collective catalogue of photos, data visualizations, and maps that link personal experiences to geospatial data, showing how different people may experience the same places differently. In addition, the collective activity generates a less tangible but more critical output as, when participants are given back their data in the form of a catalogue, they remain in charge of their materials (in terms of both data points and images).

Formatting the data collection results into visual artefacts may serve as a form of recognition of the work of those participating in digital research (as discussed above). Visual methods (specifically feminist approaches to data visualization) can also be helpful in questioning who is asked to participate in a study. Carrying out impactful and participatory work with data entails asking who is brought to the table and carefully considering who is asked to participate (D'Ignazio et al., 2021). In the 'Urban Belonging' project, participants were invited to the table by virtue of belonging to specific marginalized groups, organized

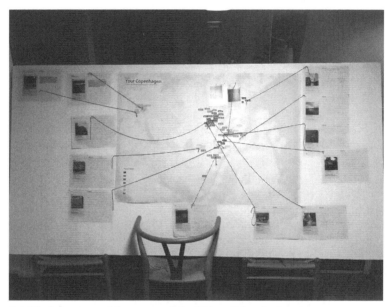

5.4 Workshop materials as part of the 'Urban Belonging' project.

in local associations. However, the participants regrouped based on where they had taken photos in the city. In addition, they are also asked whether they identify with one of the other minorities invited to the study. Were they maybe also self-identifying as disabled, international, LGBTQ+, etc.? The results of this self-identification exercise were visualized as a set of gradients on a map, with every participant represented as a multi-coloured polygon (each colour hue representing one marginalized group, and the shape representing the city's boundaries of Copenhagen according to their perception). The self-identification exercise and associated visualization method take up the challenge to 'rethink binaries and hierarchies' (D'Ignazio & Klein, 2020) and generally question traditional classification methods.

Conclusion

This chapter discusses visual methodologies and visualization strategies in relation to STS, feminist theory, and participatory (digital) research, and puts forward methods of visualization that invite public participation. While visualizations are often seen as the end product of research and are used to disseminate results, they may also facilitate collaborative research processes, aid analyses, or drive debates in participatory settings. In the tracing of debates in STS regarding public participation, knowledge production, and the role and position of the researcher therein, Latour's *matters of concern* (2007) can help researchers focus on how facts are assembled and constructed while taking care of those involved in the knowledge-making process. The evolution of participatory research can be traced to the proposal to include *matters of care* (Puig de la Bellacasa, 2011) in the study of politically charged issues. The integration of care and caution in digital research has been taken up by developing feminist perspectives on data science (D'Ignazio & Klein, 2020). In its quest for recognizing power imbalances, data feminism attends to a multiplicity of perspectives and elevates situated and embodied knowledges. Research methods that take seriously more subjective and personal approaches to issues and their situated experiences may be a good fit for studying societal challenges and debates.

When exploring what the digital turn has brought to participatory research, new concerns have been raised about the digitization of various steps of the research process. The dependency of the researcher on the limitations of digital platforms in the data collection process makes digital research a distributed effort (Marres, 2012) between users, platforms, and researchers. The entanglement of agencies and misalignments (between tools and the researcher's goal) in digital research points to new ways of thinking about digital participation. However, according to data feminist scholars, the digital turn also reinforces existing societal imbalances, which are exacerbated by technology, and lead to the exclusion of those usually uncounted in data analysis.

Looking at visualization practices, we address which roles visual formats can play in designing participation in and with the digital, and in learning from various projects that engage with various communities to produce (urban) knowledge. These experiences in public participation make use of various visual formats (composite images, tableaux, data catalogues, and cartographic maps) and create research settings where participants are asked to *talk back* to the data. In the design of these experiences, where groups of affected actors organize around data points and are invited to talk back to the visualization outputs, lies an opportunity to carry out impactful participatory research.

Further Readings

- Burgos-Thorsen, S., Niederer, S. & Koed Madsen, A. (2023). What is an inclusive city? Reconfiguring participation in planning with geospatial photovoice to unpack experiences of urban belonging among marginalized communities. *Visual Studies.* https://doi.org/10.1080/1472586X.2023.2261897.
- D'Ignazio, C. & Klein, L. F. (2020). *Data Feminism.* Cambridge, MA: MIT Press.
- Ricci, D., Calibro, Evennou, D. & Verjat, B. (2021). Developing online images: from visual traces to public voices. *Revista Diseña* (19). doi.org/10.7764/disena.19.Article.2.

6

Machine Images: Generative Visual AI for Research

This chapter introduces different ways to conduct visual research with generative AI by proposing a conceptual shift from prompt engineering to prompt design. It demonstrates techniques for exploring machine biases, content moderation policies, and ways to use generative visual AI for participatory practices.

Introduction[15]

A few days before a Manhattan grand jury indicted Donald Trump for his involvement in a scandal relating to hush-money payments, images depicting his arrest started circulating online (figure 6.1). The hyper-realistic images, showing the former president being dragged by police, were tweeted by Eliot Higgins, founder of the independent investigative collective Bellingcat. While the author clearly stated that images were AI-generated (the tweet caption reading: 'Making pictures of Trump getting arrested while waiting for Trump's arrest'), as some of the visuals started to circulate, their incredible realism shocked and even fooled less informed users, as prominent online platforms struggled to swiftly adopt measures to flag the images as misleading (Stanley-Becker & Nix, 2023).

A few days after Donald Trump's images circulated, new iconic AI-generated visuals entered the news. Posted on Reddit with the title 'The Pope Drip', the images portray Pope Francis wearing an oversized, Balenciaga-style, white puffer jacket (figure 6.2). The photographs were incredibly realistic, and although, if looked at closely, they revealed signs of their AI-generated origins, they were compelling enough to deceive even the most tech-savvy internet users (Golby, 2023), mainly when they started to circulate outside their original context. The images were shared on Reddit before being tweeted over the weekend, where many assumed they were genuine.

6.1 Generated visuals (with Midjourney) with the prompt: 'Donald Trump falling over while getting arrested. Fibonacci Spiral. News footage.'

6.2 AI-generated visuals (with Midjourney) of the Pope wearing a puffer jacket, posted on r/midjourney on Reddit by a since-deleted user.

Both sets of visuals were created using Midjourney AI, a tool that can generate photorealistic images starting from a natural-language prompt. Midjourney is just one of the many AI-powered text-to-image tools (i.e., tools that require textual input to output an image) that have recently spread exponentially. While there have been previous experiments with text-to-image generation, prior to the development of deep learning technologies, such attempts to create text-to-image models were confined to making collages from already-existing image components (Agnese et al., 2019). Working with such models entailed entering a textual query which resulted in a selection of images (or parts of these images) from a database and composing an image from these selected visuals (Zhu et al., 2007). More recent models instead generate digital images from natural-language descriptions – called 'prompts' – and do so with unprecedented sophistication.

Celebrated as a ground-breaking technology in the news, generative visual AI has entered the cultural sector and creative industries, where it is used in producing creative work, news imagery, animation, and other cultural endeavours. When, in April 2022, OpenAI announced DALL-E 2 (a more advanced generative model), various news magazines used an AI-powered generative tool to design their cover, the image paired with celebratory titles such as 'How a computer designed this week's cover' (*The Economist*, 2022) and 'The world's smartest Artificial Intelligence just made its first magazine cover' (Liu, 2022).

The refinement of the generated outputs (and the ease with which they can be produced) has also shaken up the art world. For example, a generated image (with Midjourney) won first place in the digital art competition at the 2022 Colorado State Fair (Gault, 2022), sparking controversy among fellow artists, questioning the ownership of the artwork. Debates about ownership of the generated visuals meld with those about the copyright of the images used to train these systems. For example, Stable Diffusion (another text-to-image model) is trained on LAION-5B, a data set of more than 2 billion images (and associated captions) scraped from the public web (Beaumont, 2022). An analysis of a small subset of the data set (Baio, 2022) has found numerous images scraped from databases that hold copyrighted images, such as Flickr, DeviantArt, and Tumblr, and even stock photo sites such as Getty Images and Shutterstock. The presence of copyrighted images is also noticeable from the program's tendency to reproduce the Getty Images watermark in some images (figure 6.3), often when the prompt includes the phrase 'news photo'.

6.3 Images with the prompt 'Old donald trump behind the bars in a jail, news photo', with a 'GettyImages' watermark overlaid automatically by the text-to-image tool.

Training sets containing (copyrighted) images from online art communities such as DeviantArt have resulted in the ability of these systems to mimic the 'style and aesthetics of living artists' (Vincent, 2022), which presents an ethical and possibly legal issue. One can indeed prompt any description, and adding 'in the style of' will mimic the style of the mentioned artist. The issue has led to lawsuits in the US, where artists have sued AI companies, as images imitating the signature styles of particular artists 'are already sold on the internet, siphoning commissions from the artists themselves' (Feldman, 2023). The question that is raised is whether the signature style should also be copyrighted (and not only the images themselves), for the machine has learned the style from artists who are 'missing out on profits' (Feldman, 2023). In response to this concern, computer software company Adobe has developed its own in-house model (dubbed Adobe Firefly), which claims to be only trained on licensed images and public domain content whose copyright has expired (Wadhwani, 2023).

This chapter asks what kind of research one can do with machine-generated visuals, proposing a shift from prompt engineering to prompt design. Prompt engineering, as we refer to current prompting practices, is about mastering the art of prompting to generate awe-inducing images: perfect renderings, surprising remixes, or absurd-yet-realistic images. On the other hand, prompt design entails formulating prompts for cultural and visual research (including research on bias, AI aesthetics, machine critique, content moderation, and participatory research).

First, we survey different prompt engineering practices, noting a shift from earlier prompting, aimed at testing the limits of the new technology, to prompt optimization and prompting becoming a (commercial) service. With prompt optimization there also comes a shift from natural-language descriptions (as prompts are advertised) to machine language, with prompt engineers composing long, complex prompts that look more like a line of code. Second, we move from prompt engineering to prompt design, discussing ways to prompt generative visual AI for research purposes. Here, we outline different strategies, including generic prompts for bias research, prompting and counter-prompting, evocative prompting, provocative prompting for content moderation research, reverse-engineered prompting for machine critique, and abstract prompting for public participatory settings. In all, the chapter offers a conceptual and applied agenda for critical research with generative visual AI.

What's the prompt for this?
On prompt engineering

Arguably, the most substantive innovation in generative visual AI lies in the novel form of user input it requires, which shifts from having to master a graphical interface (GUI) to text-based (TUI) input, as the software accepts descriptions expressed in natural language – called prompts – and turns them into images. Naming the instruction as a prompt might be read as a marketing move, as it anthropomorphizes the machine: one *stimulates* the creativity of the generative system, which is prompted, rather than inputted, as one would do when feeding data into a computer.

Prompting, in its original meaning, helps humans to get unstuck and release their creativity. The *New Oxford American Dictionary* (2023) defines prompting as 'an act of encouraging a hesitating speaker', as in 'with barely a prompt, Barbara talked on'. In the theatre, the prompter cues actors when they forget their lines or are misplaced on the stage (in French and other languages, the prompter is called 'souffleur', as the lines are quietly whispered to get the actor back on track) (figure 6.4). Prompts may be used for creative writing, essay writing, and other written work, in the form of a phrase, paragraphs, or images that serve as direction and motivation. The *New York Times* publishes a daily prompt for students inspired by its content (*The New York Times* – The Learning Network, n.d.), and writing contests may publish a prompt in their call for submissions. There are also drawing prompts, which consist of textual descriptions of subjects to be painted to stimulate the uninspired artist. Such drawing prompts can be simple keywords (wind, vegetables, books) or more detailed descriptions (a heart containing your childhood memories), and they might be compiled into collections to choose from for daily practice (Hill, n.d.).

With generative AI, prompting becomes a skill to be honed. Prompt engineering, as the task is called, is a matter of matching input with output 'to get the most interesting outcomes' (Bridle,

6.4 Milivoje Nikolić (1904–?), whisperer and actor, in the prompt box, National Theatre of the Danube Banovina, 1939.

2023). The prompter – or 'prompt engineer' – masters the skill of 'framing' instructions 'in terms most clearly understood by the system, so it returns the results that most closely match expectations – or perhaps exceed them' (Bridle, 2023). The skill of prompt engineering is also tool-specific – that is, the prompt is adapted to the machine. The prompt engineer needs to cultivate sensitivity towards different systems and how they interpret the same input, as one prompt that is fed into different tools will yield different results (Monge, 2022).

If prompting is a skill that requires know-how, it might as well be showcased and turned into a performance: 'Do you have what it takes to become a Prompt Engineer?' (Schmidt & Schmieg, n.d.). During a prompt battle (Screen Walks, 2022), as the format is called, contestants compete live to compile the perfect prompt to generate the most interesting image according to given tasks ('recreate the following image', 'place yourself into a Hollywood movie of your choice', 'OpenAI won't be happy about the image you are about to create next'). These battles may occur online but also offline, and letting the crowd judge the created work and vote by walking across the room to stand behind the winner.

Stressing the machine: testing AI capabilities with remix prompts

What does one prompt AI for? Although the tech is relatively new, one can observe a shift from the earlier prompting, aimed at testing the machine's capabilities (and limitations), towards the optimization of prompting, which comes with guides, tutorials, and cheat sheets. In early work with generative visual AI, we see prompts formulated to let the machine produce absurd images, leaving its viewers in awe and admiration for what the technology can do. As the new models do not simply work by compiling parts of images from the training set but instead generate new ones from scratch, prompting aims at producing coherent and realistic visuals of chimerical subjects, liberally combining clashing styles and subjects into one image. Showcased in collections on subreddits and Twitter profiles, the race is to compose the prompt that generates the most absurd combinations of settings, concepts, and depictions, such as 'Donald Trump as the baby from the Nevermind album cover' or 'Freddie Mercury eating ramen inside a washing machine' (figure 6.5). The tools themselves market the technology for its imaginative power, inviting the users to prompt 'unrelated concepts' which 'are unlikely to exist in the real world' (OpenAI, 2021). The original splash page of DALL-E offered examples such as 'A snail with the texture of a harp' or 'An armchair in the shape of an avocado'.

Prompt optimization and commodification: prompt guides, prompt tutorials, and prompting as a (commercial) service

While prompts can be 'lazy' (Ekenstam, 2023a), composed of the minimum required to get what one needs, a 'good prompt' should be as specific and detailed as possible, according to

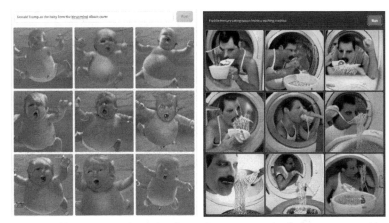

6.5 Donald Trump as the baby from the Nevermind album cover; Freddie Mercury eating ramen inside a washing machine.

growing literature on prompt engineering (figure 6.6). As prompt engineering is presented as an art that needs to be mastered, guides and tools for prompt optimization are being developed and marketed. Prompt books, continuously updated, focus on prompt formats, effective modifiers, and even 'magic words' (Open Art, 2022). With prompt engineering, the new genre of 'prompt optimization' arises, complete with video tutorials on YouTube, guides, cheat sheets on Substack, and experts sharing the tricks of the trade on Twitter.

As prompting evolves into a commercial service, there is also a comeback of the graphical interface. Prompting tools, designed to help users compose more effective and detailed prompts, provide a graphical layer that simplifies the process and enhances user experience. One example is PromptPerfect, whose promise is to 'elevate prompts to perfection' (Jina AI GmbH, 2023). Given a prompt, the tool adds details and streamlines it to be interpreted correctly by the different systems available (including DALL-E 2, Stable Diffusion, and Midjourney).

From natural language to machine language: structured, dynamic, negative, and weighted prompts

With optimization, prompt engineering – aside from the re-entry of the graphical interface – also shifts back from natural to

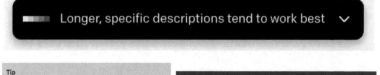

6.6 Screenshots from text-to-image websites invite the prompt to be detailed and specific.

machine language. The professionalization of prompting moves the input away from a descriptive sentence, as detailed as it might be, towards a complex string of characters. While prompting is marketed as the art of inputting descriptions in natural language, the most advanced prompts are more similar to strings of code with their specific syntax (e.g., tags divided by commas, parentheses, and hyphens). The more skilled the prompter is, the less the prompt will look like 'raw text' (Nielsen, 2023) and the more it will resemble a line of code. Prompts become structured, dynamic (allowing for debugging), negative, and even weighted.

Structured prompting is a way of composing a prompt as an array of tags (rather than as a complete sentence). Structured prompts break down the composition of the text input into components (or variables, to borrow a term from coding) such as type, camera angle, colour palette, texture, mood, and time of day. Relatedly, Stable Diffusion suggests composing a prompt from categories such as subject, medium, style, artist, website, resolution, additional details, colour, and lighting (Stable Diffusion Art, 2023a). Adobe Firefly offers the possibility to choose from a pre-defined set of features (including content type, styles, lighting, and composition) through a graphical interface. The collective Domestic Data Streamers have published a guide to 'build data visualisation through AI' (Domestic Data Streamers, 2022), which helps break down the prompt into 'quantitative semantic fields', such as density (going from 'extremely sparse' to 'extremely dense'), quantity, size (micro, tiny, big, huge, gigantic), distance, and glossiness. This structured prompting can also be put to use for debugging in a process referred to as dynamic prompting. Here, one changes a single keyword from the prompt at a time in an iterative process to discern what visual feature it controls.

Negative prompting is a way to tweak the prompt by means of removal instead of addition: 'If you see something you don't want, put it in a negative prompt' (Stable Diffusion Art, 2023a). It is a pursuit of precision that works not only with descriptions of what an image should contain but also with descriptions of what it should not. Negative prompts might be used for different goals, such as removing things (adding 'people' as a negative prompt will remove persons from a crowded scene) or modifying images (adding 'windy' to a negative prompt will turn floating hair still in a portrait). Negative prompting might also be used to tweak the style of the generated visuals: the negative prompt 'painting, cartoon' makes the result more photo-like, and 'bad art, beginner, amateur' forces the tool to pick styles in the training data set from trending artists. In this last application, negative prompting can be considered a way to interface with the training set of the model, as one excludes keywords thinking about what might be included in the training. There are even tag lists that might be used as negative prompts to generally improve the quality of the output (figure 6.7). 'Poorly drawn hands' may be a striking example thereof, targeting one of the weak spots of earlier generative visual AI. The practice, dubbed 'universal negative prompting', is reminiscent of hashtag dumps used on Instagram to boost the popularity of a post.

Finally, with weighted prompts, the input moves further away from a natural-language caption and increasingly looks more like a string of code, with formalized syntax, punctuation, and variables, rather than words. Weighting prompts refers to the possibility of adding modifiers to increase or decrease the importance of certain keywords: 'using () in prompt increases model's attention to enclosed words, and [] decreases it' (Stable Diffusion, 2023). Although prompt weighting makes the input more like a line of code, it also foregrounds the limits of the text-based approach to generating visuals, as weighting a prompt is

> ugly, tiling, poorly drawn hands, poorly drawn feet, poorly drawn face, out of frame, extra limbs, disfigured, deformed, body out of frame, bad anatomy, watermark, signature, cut off, low contrast, underexposed, overexposed, bad art, beginner, amateur, distorted face

6.7 Universal negative prompt lists suggested by Stable Diffusion to improve contrast and exposition and avoid common issues that might appear in the generated visual.

just like moving a (graphical) slider left and right, as one would do with a graphical interface.

As discussed, prompt engineering aims to create both the ultimate image and the perfect prompt and moves the generative visual AI back to a graphical interface and machine (rather than natural) language. In what follows, we argue that prompting for research requires a shift from prompt engineering towards prompt design. We will also discuss and illustrate several approaches for prompt design for generative visual AI that can be used in digital and participatory research.

Prompts as queries: from prompt engineering to prompt design

In our discussion of prompt engineering, we have seen that the term and the practice have focused on mastering the skill of prompting to generate awe-inducing, surprising images (by combining unrelated keywords and clashing styles and concepts) or 'perfect' images, where the prompts are so elaborately formulated – and possibly even tool-enhanced and systematically debugged – that all elements of surprise are eliminated. In tandem with the race towards the perfect output runs the quest for the perfect prompt, and services and how-tos are created to aid the underskilled prompter to become a skilful prompt engineer.

However, when using generative visual AI for visual, digital, and participatory research, we propose a shift from prompt engineering to 'prompt design'. With prompt design, one seeks to compose prompts as queries, in line with digital methods work on 'query design' (Rogers, 2017) when developing strategies of 'search as research'. Where search as research is about developing queries for social and cultural research with platform content and search engine results, prompt design is about developing conceptual and applied research strategies for critical inquiry with generative visual AI. Different prompting techniques include formulating ambiguous generic prompts for bias research, experimenting with prompting and 'counterprompting', provocative prompting for content moderation research, evocative prompting, reverse-engineered prompting for machine critique, and abstract prompting for elicitation purposes in participatory settings. In all, the chapter offers a conceptual and applied agenda for critical research with generative visual AI.

Ambiguous prompting for visual bias research

Like any other AI system (see chapter 4), text-to-image tools are not exempt from racially and gender-biased results or issues of over and under-representation (Bianchi et al., 2022; Nicoletti & Bass, 2023). The training sets used to build the technology (i.e., labelled image databases) affect the diversity of the generated outputs, giving rise to various kinds of (more or less subtle) bias. As it is trained on multimodal data sets (Birhane et al., 2021), which pair images with text, the question is whether the system will generate discriminatory, racial, and gendered images when prompted with certain terms.

For example, it has been demonstrated how DALL-E 2 perpetuates gender stereotypes, mainly related to professions – such as generating higher numbers of men than women for prompts that do not mention gender (Strickland, 2022). OpenAI has since implemented mitigation techniques for producing outputs that 'more accurately reflect the diversity of the world's population' (OpenAI, 2022b), in particular when the system receives a prompt that describes a person whose race or gender is not specified, such as 'firefighter'. The problem has no quick fix, though, as it is speculated that such mitigation techniques merely involve adding 'either male or female or Black, Asian or Caucasian' (Traylor, 2022) randomly in the back end to prompts that do not mention race or gender. There have also been attempts to develop generative models that respond to such issues. For example, MissJourney is an indipendent AI generator that exclusively generates images featuring women when prompted with profession types (TEDxAmsterdam Women, 2023).

In addition to the concerns regarding gender and race, some have noted how these systems exhibit Western-centric behaviour, meaning that they over-represent Western concepts, styles, and traditions. For instance, DALL-E 2 tends to assume Western traditions when prompted with generic terms such as 'wedding', 'restaurant', or 'home' (OpenAI, 2022a). The overrepresentation of Western images (in the training sets and, consequently, in the generated output) shows even through human expressions. When asked to generate a selfie of soldiers and warriors from various periods and geographic locations, Midjourney renders historically accurate depictions with a homogeneous smile, which for some is a typical Western facial expression (as the system is trained on Western selfies). The behaviour might be read as American culture colonizing facial expressions, as 'the diversity of human expression' does not 'survive algorithmic hegemony' (Gurfinkel, 2023). Western-centrism is also acknowledged on the prompt side: given that the systems are trained on English-captioned images, descriptions in other languages will generate worse and less accurate results. Stable Diffusion claims to perform worse with prompts expressed in languages other than English (Rombach & Esser, 2022).

In a research setting, the generated visual is more than just an object to be evaluated for its plausibility (e.g., the extent to which it is impossible to distinguish a human-made one from a machine-generated one) or remarkability. Instead, these generated images could be considered as 'infographics about the dataset' (Salvaggio, 2022), where the 'dataset' here refers to the model's training set. This research outlook melds the prompt with the generated output and the training set: one seeks to compose a prompt that enables one to observe the bias in the training data set by analysing the generated output. This can be considered a visual strategy in the tradition of so-called 'algorithmic auditing', developed for the 'public scrutiny' of the algorithms that underpin our infrastructures and 'provide functions like social sorting, market segmentation, personalization, recommendations, and the management of traffic flows from bits to cars' (Sandvig et al., 2014, p. 3).

Visual bias research moves the task of prompting away from the quest for specificity (as suggested by prompt books and optimization tutorials) towards more ambiguity. When prompting for machine auditing, one strives for a certain level of vagueness and designs the prompt to be as generic as possible (as opposed to long and detailed) to let the generative machine fill in the gaps. Such ambiguity enables the researcher to test how the machine was trained. As one would do when querying search engines with ambiguous queries, generic prompting is a way to appeal to the machine's ability to fill in the blanks as well as disambiguate the terminology. In the aforementioned context of 'search as research' (Rogers, 2013), which seeks to repurpose search engine results for social and cultural research, one would query Google Search for ambiguous terms, such as 'rights', and rely on the search engine's ability to specify the term and 'create hierarchies of concerns', employing Google as a 'socio-epistemological machine' (Rogers, 2017a). Relatedly, an ambiguous prompt (e.g., prompting 'firefighter' without specifying the gender) pushes the generative system, which is asked to 'disambiguate' the action, term, or concept to fill in for the lack of detail

Indeed, the distinction between an ambiguous and unambiguous query – the latter being 'one in which it is clear which results one is after' (Rogers, 2017a, p. 87) – also holds for prompting. With prompt engineering and optimization, one knows what one is after. Therefore, the task is to compose a less ambiguous and more detailed prompt to control the result, matching expectations with outputs (Bridle, 2023). Conversely, with generic prompting, the researcher is vague on purpose, inviting the generative machine to fill in the blanks. Ambiguous (or generic) prompting also builds on the tendency of the system to give back a result, whatever the prompt (even with prompts that are not clear, not specific, or even nonsensical). In a research setting, these *mansplaining* tendencies (Harrison, 2023) of AI technologies can be put to use in research that aims to test its bias.

In a project examining how a machine (in this case, Stable Diffusion) visualizes climate effects and solutions, generic prompting is used to expose the lack of diversity in AI-generated visuals for climate-change-related topics (Cattaneo et al., 2023). Rather than prompting 'people cycling through a city', one prompts a generic sentence such as 'people engaging in sustainable activities' without mentioning the activity. The output foregrounds a narrow interpretation of sustainability (figure 6.8), as the system consistently generates images of tree-planting scenes (and the occasional bicycle out of context).

Ambiguous prompting for visual bias research is applied programmatically in the tool 'Stable Diffusion Bias Explorer' (Luccioni, 2022). The interface prompts professions and adjectives in order to inquire how the system (initially limited to Stable Diffusion but later expanded to others, such as DALL-E) represents different professions and adjectives (figure 6.9). The interface juxtaposes the two results, allowing for quick comparison and 'to see firsthand how the AI model maps' professions and descriptive

6.8 The consistent output depicting people gardening generated by Stable Diffusion when prompted with 'people engaging in sustainable activities'.

terms 'to racial and gender stereotypes' (Rose, 2022). For example, when prompting professions such as director, doctor, or software developer, the AI model consistently depicts men, whereas prompting professions such as 'nurse' or 'social worker' generates women. The tool also foregrounds 'stark differences in what types of faces the model generates based on what descriptors are used' (Rose, 2022). For instance, prompting 'CEO' almost always returns an image of a man, 'but is more likely to generate women if the accompanying adjectives are terms like supportive and compassionate' (Rose, 2022).

In a project looking at how generative visual AI mediates the issue of biodiversity, ambiguous prompting is employed to explore (lack of) diversity in how 'biodiversity' is known and imagined by AI (Colombo et al., 2023). The term 'biodiversity' is prompted in different generative visual AI (i.e., Midjourney, Stable Diffusion, DALL-E, Craiyon, Dream, Lexica, and Adobe Firefly), and five generated images per model are selected. The output, where images are displayed and described, reveals

6.9 Stable Diffusion-generated visuals for the prompts 'CEO' (left) and 'social worker' (right), juxtaposed in the interface of Stable Diffusion Bias Explorer (Luccioni, 2022). The results show how the prompt 'CEO' generates images of men, while the prompt 'social worker' generates women.

recurrent themes and styles in the representation of biodiversity (both across models and model-specific). Generally, each model returns an idealized and stereotypical depiction of biodiversity (figure 6.10). Even when the prompt does not specify a location, biodiversity is mainly associated with tropical landscapes and species rather than ordinary nature. In addition, each model positively frames biodiversity in the present: the human degradation or decline of biodiversity is not depicted in any of the images, and humans are absent from the images.

The project also focuses on animal species and their relative prominence in relation to different geographical areas, asking: which species are foregrounded and which are left out? Are there differences in the species represented for the topic of biodiversity across geographical regions? To this end, the prompt 'biodiversity' is combined with the names of different continents. The generated visuals (with Midjourney) are then collected, and all prominent animals and insects in the pictures are cut out. The cut-out animals are then laid flat in the shape of the continents to compose a world map (figure 6.11).

The world map shows how biodiversity is associated with different species on different continents and how, in some cases, certain species dominate the continent. For example, Antarctica is solely populated by penguins, and South America by colourful tropical birds. North America comprises butterflies, eagle-like birds, and some hybrid mammals. Oceania is about fish and birds. The continents of Africa, Europe, and Asia show the most diversity in animal species. Africa features elephants, zebras, giraffes, and a flock of birds. Europe holds mostly birds, butterflies, and some mammals, including platypus. Asia shows diverse animals, from tigers and elephants to birds and butterflies. Apart from geographical differences, the world map exposes how only certain species (and specific animals) are associated with the concept of biodiversity, as birds and butterflies appear to be the most prominent species across continents, and the only insects that appear on the map are butterflies.

Prompting and counter-prompting for bias research

In addition to generic (or ambiguous) prompts, one other approach to machine bias research is prompting and counter-prompting, which entails prompting opposite sentences (or

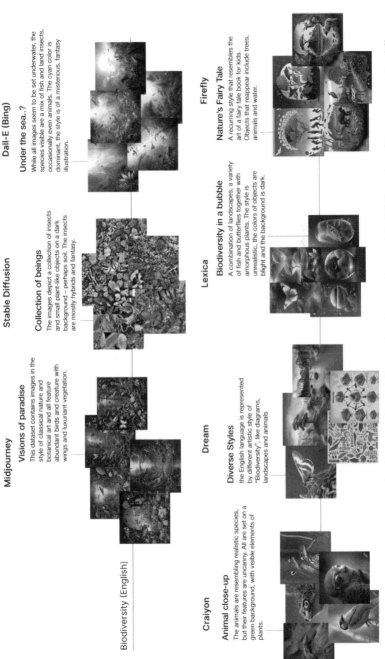

Dall-E (Bing)

Under the sea..?

While all images seem to be set underwater, the species visible are a mix of fish and land insects, occasionally even animals. The cyan color is dominant, the style is of a misterious, fantasy illustration.

Firefly

Nature's Fairy Tale

A recurring style that resembles the art of a fairy tale book for kids. Objects that reappear include trees, animals and water.

Stable Diffusion

Collection of beings

The images depict a collection of insects and small plant-like objects on a dark background – perhaps soil. The insects are mostly hybrids and fantasy.

Lexica

Biodiversity in a bubble

A combination of landscapes, a variety of fish and butterflies together with amorphous plants. The style is unrealistic, the colors of objects are blight and the background is dark.

Midjourney

Visions of paradise

This dataset contains images in the style of classical nature and botanical art and all feature abundant birds and creature with wings and luxuriant vegetation.

Dream

Diverse Styles

the English language is represented by different artistic style of "Biodiversity", like diagrams, landscapes and animals

Craiyon

Animal close-up

The animals are resembling realistic species, but their features are uncanny. All are set on a green background, with visible elements of plants.

Biodiversity (English)

6.10 Generated visuals for the prompt 'biodiversity' from different visual generative models. While styles of images are quite different, the overall interpretation of the issue is similar across models, with biodiversity framed as a tropical abundance of (non-human) beings.

6.11 World map composed of cut-outs of animals extracted from visuals generated by Midjourney for the prompt 'biodiversity in' + [name of the continent]. Source: Colombo et al. (2023).

terms) that would distil the bias in the visual representation of competing concepts. The research approach recalls the notion of queries as side-taking keywords, as they can be part of 'programmes or anti-programmes', where 'programmes refer to efforts made at putting forward and promoting a particular proposal, campaign or project', and 'anti-programmes oppose these efforts or projects through keywords' (Rogers, 2017a, p. 83). When formulating a query, one considers how keywords may advance or oppose a particular agenda 'to study trends, commitments and alignments between actors' (Rogers, 2017a). An example is querying Google Image Search with two contrasting terms used to refer to the Israeli–Palestinian barrier ('apartheid wall' versus 'security fence') and comparing the results to tease out opposing narratives: one depicting 'graffitied, wall-like structures, barbed wire, protests, and people being somehow excluded'; the other showing 'lightweight, high-tech structures' (Rogers, 2017a, p. 89). Relatedly, with prompting and counter-prompting, one may compose sentences that refer to the same issue but are formulated with different wording to compare contrasting worldviews and opposite or competing perspectives.

Evocative prompting

Similar to ambiguous prompting, where a generative AI model is invited to share its interpretation of an action or actor, machine testing might even be taken further by evocative prompting (formulating a prompt that includes non-existing evocative terms). As generative AI will always produce something (except for banned terms, as discussed in the following section on provocative prompting), users can prompt fictional words and observe the results. As such, evocative prompts enable the user to peek into the training sets and even audit the mechanisms of the visual generation.

One notable case is 'Crungus', a made-up word found to return consistent visuals when prompted repeatedly. Prompting the 'otherwise unknown phrase' in DALL-E mini (the free, lighter version of the tool from OpenAI) repeatedly generates images of a 'snarling, naked, ogre-like figure' (Bridle, 2023). The word has no visual historical reference – thus, it can be said to be entirely imagined by the machine. The case is also telling of a broader tendency of generative AIs to always return an output, whatever the input. The behaviour has earned Chat GPT (the chatbot developed by OpenAI) the nickname of 'mansplaining machine', owing to its inclination of always giving answers at the cost of inventing facts: 'often wrong, and yet always certain' (Harrison, 2023). Relatedly, the new, more advanced Chat GPT-4 is advertised as 'less likely to invent facts' (Hern & Bhuiyan, 2023), which reveals how fabrication was present in earlier versions.

Provocative prompting for content moderation research

Issues of misinformation and offensive and biased results have sparked debates on (the failing of) moderation policies of text-to-image generation tools and generative AI more broadly. The standards (also related to violent and sexual imagery) for what is acceptable to generate, the strictness by which such standards are enforced, and the technique for moderating results vary significantly between the tools.

One moderation technique is prompt filtering (OpenAI, 2022a), which entails filtering some keywords for which the system will not return any result. The technique is weak: prompt-based filtering is easy to bypass using alternative terms that result in a similar output. These are referred to as 'visual synonyms' (Gavves et al., 2012) and might be used to circumvent the filter, as one prompts objects or concepts visually similar to those that are filtered, such as including ketchup to replace blood.

The question with moderation is what a system allows users to generate (or not). DALL-E's rules include a ban on creating images that are 'not G-rated, or that could cause harm' (OpenAI, 2022c) and comes with a list of prohibited topics, such as hateful content, violence, or sexual content. The system also blocks prompts that are related to 'major conspiracies or events related to major ongoing geopolitical events' (OpenAI, 2022c) and politicians. The question is which politicians can be prompted and which cannot, and the findings might reveal political hierarchies.

Midjourney has a list of banned terms, constantly updated, crowd-sourced, and country-specific, as the list contains terms 'related to topics in different countries based on complaints from users in those countries' (Midjourney, 2022). For example, the term 'arrested' has been added to the list after visuals of Donald Trump's arrest circulated widely. The fact that the list is up to date (rather than settled) enables a form of longitudinal analysis, as one could systematically conduct provocative prompting over time and see which terms remain blocked and which are allowed back again.

Stable Diffusion takes a looser approach. Founder and CEO Mostaque states that 'ultimately, it's peoples' responsibility as to whether they are ethical, moral, and legal in how they operate this technology' (Vincent, 2022). While the interface tool has built-in keyword filters (such as 'nazi'), the model is open source, and one can run it on a personal machine and circumvent these limitations (Vincent, 2022). Following the model's release to the general public, a number of subreddits devoted to collecting the NSFW (short for 'not safe for work') output of the software appeared, now mostly banned (Cole, 2022).

The varying degrees of looseness by which different models enforce content moderation might be audited by prompting sensitive keywords to ascertain which model blocks them and which does not. The research process might start with compiling a list of prompts (such as thematic keywords or political figures) and inputting them into different models to characterize and compare their content moderation policy (in terms of general strictness, but also compared by topic).

Comparative reverse-engineered prompting for machine critique and trend research

Prompting can be seen as an attempt to query the training set. Prompt engineers seek to include in their prompts terms that might stir the machine to pick content and styles from a particular subset of the training set. For example, adding 'trending on Behance' to the prompt will generate high-quality, sharp images that mimic the platform's top-voted content style. More recently, there are tools and techniques for reverse engineering a prompt starting from a (AI-generated or otherwise created) visual. CLIP Interrogator helps the prompter 'figure out what a good prompt might be to create new images like an existing one' (pharmapsychotic, 2023). With the tool, one uploads an image, learns how the model would describe the image, and can replicate the result. On Midjourney, one can generate a textual description (formatted as a prompt) with the feature '/describe' (DelSignore, 2023).

These features can be used to research the multimodal nature of generative visual AI, where images and text are closely intertwined (i.e., labelled or captioned images in the training sets behind the model for generative visuals). How would a system write a prompt for a particular image? Similar to research that characterizes different computer vision systems by comparing labels for the same set of images (as briefly discussed in chapter 2), with reverse-engineered prompts, one could audit the generative systems, in a cross-model analysis, by feeding the same image to different models and comparing the suggested prompts. Is a model skewed towards a particular kind of word? Do different models each speak a (slightly) different language? The findings would enable the characterization of the models and offer a glimpse of the images (and captions) used in the training.

In addition, one can employ reverse-engineered prompting for trend research. Instead of adding keywords to the prompt to obtain a particular style (as prompt engineers do), one can reverse-engineer the prompts to see which styles emerge or are more prominent. For example, in the project concerning biodiversity and visual AI described before (Colombo et al., 2023), reverse engineering prompts from visuals about biodiversity consistently returned the phrase 'Shutterstock contest winner', hinting at what kind of visuals the generative systems were trained on.

Abstract prompting for public participatory settings

In the previous strategies for visual research with generative AI, prompts were designed to work either with or against the machine to research its workings and underlying training. In this last strategy, prompts are designed for public participatory settings. Where ambiguous and generic prompts can be used to let the machine reveal its training sets and logic, abstract prompting can also be used in speculative settings to create images that can, in turn, become visual prompts for (human) speculation or reflection.

In a science communications project aimed to let school children and their caregivers reflect on the implications of sea-level rise for the Netherlands,[16] researchers decided to invite the school children to take a picture of their surroundings (for example, their street, their sports club, or their school), and imagine what this would look like in the year 2100. Using geographic knowledge from their geography class on sea-level rise and their imagination, the students were invited to overlay the image with abstract 'filters' to indicate floods, heavy weather, and other elements, and eventually to annotate the collage with some lines of text.

To create the filters (figure 6.12), the researchers designed prompts to generate images that were evocative enough to be enticing but vague enough so that participants could project their thoughts, feelings, and associations, which may vary across participants, as with responses to the ink blots in a Rorschach test. The prompts lead to a first set of images that are presented to experts, who reviewed the images and added suggestions for more specific ones (e.g., of possible situations in the future affected by climate change, including heavy rain, storms, wildfire, people together, running away, sheltering, animals and vegetation, wild animals, and infrastructures).

After the final set of images was generated, visuals were transformed into filters with Adobe Photoshop by flattening the colours and making them usable as overlays on black-and-white photographs (figure 6.13). In this example, prompting was done to generate a catalogue of visual elements that could function as prompts (for humans). The visual elements in the filters are the opposite of data visualization or isotype (as developed by Otto Neurathi), as they are not meant to be a complete visual system that represents each individual element. Rather than the

6.12 Catalogue of filters (excerpt), generated with AI by Carlo De Gaetano for the 'After us the deluge' project.

6.13 The filters are used to overlay black-and-white images.

simplification or reduction needed to visualize complex data, the images generated here shift in meaning according to each use and aim to open the issue to further reflection.

Conclusion

This chapter has outlined a conceptual and practical research agenda for generative visual AI, focusing on prompt design. First, we focused on prompting and how this practice has evolved in the realm of prompt engineering, noting a shift from earlier forms aimed at testing the limits of the technology by prompting impossible subjects to the optimization and commodification of prompting, which became a service offered through guides, tools, and tutorials teaching the unskilled prompter to generate perfect images (according to the instructions). We then contrasted prompt engineering with prompt design, offering space for critical research-driven approaches to algorithmic auditing, machine critique, and the productive use of AI for participatory settings. The distinction between prompt engineering and prompt design lies in the goal for which prompts are formulated (and their expected visual results). Prompt engineering can be described as mastering the art of prompting to generate awe-inducing images: perfect renderings, surprising remixes, or absurd-yet-realistic subjects. If prompt engineering is about controlling the results and matching the textual input with the expected output, prompt design is about formulating prompts for cultural and visual research, exploring critical research-driven use of AI.

As this chapter revolves around prompt design, the focus is on how to generate images for critical research, rather than on (visual) methods to analyse them. But after the data collection process (or, in this case, data generation), images can and should be analysed. Generated images might be analytically displayed – for instance, they can be organized by similarity and observed with a distant-reading approach (as illustrated in chapter 2), or even collectively discussed and annotated in participatory settings (as discussed in chapter 5). As generated images become ubiquitous in our visual digital culture, used in online news websites (in place of stock photography) and circulating on social media platforms, the success of some of these images (and not others) can also be an object of study. Following the social life of AI-generated images may become another approach to studying visual bias (as we do in chapter 4) or to simply looking at their resonance in different online platforms, following a networked approach to image analysis (chapter 3).

In conclusion, we want to zoom out and discuss the implications for society of the increasingly high use of generative visual AI and the role that visual research can take in this scenario. As we write this chapter (especially since the launch of DALL-E and ChatGPT in 2022), generative AI is causing tremendous hype.

Developers and researchers are grappling with the implications of the technologies, and over 27,500 of them have already signed an open letter to call for a 'temporary pause of at least 6 months' in the 'training of AI systems more powerful than GPT-4' (Future of Life Institute, 2023). Indeed, many cultural industries (journalism, film production, and other creative products) have already been affected by generative visual AI, sparking protest and inducing panic. In July 2023, Hollywood actors and writers started a joint strike, seeing in the rise of generative AI technology an 'existential threat to their livelihoods' (Pulliam-Moore, 2023), while production companies such as Netflix and Disney are investing massively in the technology (Klippenstein, 2023). The film industry is just one example of the many sectors that are (or soon will be) affected by the rise of generative AI.

While protests, strikes, and signed letters are a signal of an understandable panic that generative AI is causing, there have also been (more or less critical) responses to the growth of the technology from the art and design fields, as well as from various academic sectors. The best-known response to AI's rise and far-reaching impact in the realm of art and research already dates back to 2018, with the drawing of the anatomy of an AI system (Crawford & Joler, 2018). The work maps the extractivist inscriptions of an AI system (in this case, the worlds connected to the virtual assistant Alexa) and traces them beyond their technological stack 'into capital, labor and nature' to make visible the 'true costs of these systems – social, environmental, economic, and political –' that as of yet 'remain hidden and may stay that way for some time'. In 2023, researchers published an online repository AI featuring a 'Critical field guide for working with machine learning data sets', offering practical approaches to critical AI research. In 2019, media theorist Lev Manovich turned his attention to AI to explore its aesthetics (see Manovich, 2019), and, more recently, he has started using generative visual AI as a medium with which he creates images, and is working towards a documentary film, a book, and an exhibition.

Indeed, the recent developments in AI have both caused alarm and sparked inspiration. In addition to the risks of automation in various cultural sectors, and issues of bias and discrimination in the generated outputs, the improvement and moderation of these (primarily Western) systems heavily rely on underpaid (human) workers, who are tasked with the identification and tagging of violent, biased, and illegal content within the training data sets (Steyerl, 2023). Moreover, while the energy cost of a single AI model is hard to estimate, generative AI models (when they are developed, but also when they are used) are extremely energy-consuming, raising questions of sustainability (Saenko, 2023). In tandem with these critical concerns comes its use as a creative tool, from the prompt engineering approach of formulating the perfect prompt to critical prompting that illustrates the models' reliance on existing cultural artefacts. Another avenue that we find interesting is that of researching generative AI through the use of AI, just as we study platform images along with the platforms that host and present them. As such, we aim to produce informed critiques on this technology, for which we find it essential to use, test, and stress it.

Further Readings

- Ciston, S. (2022). A critical fieldguide for working with machine learning datasets. Knowing Machines. https://knowingmachines.org/critical-field-guide.
- Crawford, K. (2021). *Atlas of AI: Power, Politics and the Planetary Costs of Artificial Intelligence*. New Haven, CT: Yale University Press – see 'Data' chapter (pp. 89–122).
- Salvaggio, E. (2023). Critical topics: AI images. www.cyberneticforests.com/ai-images.
- Steyerl, H. (2023). 'Mean images'. *New Left Review*, 140/141, 82–97. https://newleftreview.org/issues/ii140/articles/hito-steyerl-mean-images.

Conclusion

Considering Visual Methods for Digital Research

Images have made it to the foreground of digital culture and have made a mark on a wide range of research practices. This book outlines a collection of approaches for research with images, from large sets of digital content to small sets of the most engaging social media images, and from researching bias in algorithms and machine training sets to inviting different publics into participatory research. Traditionally, visual methodologies, as a field of study that specializes in research with visual materials, has concerned itself with the study of images – their production, meaning, circulation, and reception – and the use of images as tools and instruments for research. When situating the book, we consider it an attempt to contribute to the fields of visual methodologies, where we bring more attention to digital research, to digital methods – to which we offer a singular focus on image research – as well as controversy mapping – to which we offer participatory and critical practices, and discuss the strategies of visualization that suit them most. We pay homage to many adjacent fields in this book, from data feminism and data justice to digital sociology and issue mapping. Furthermore, our backgrounds in art, media studies, communication design, and digital research shine through in the examples and approaches listed throughout the book.

This book outlines both visual methods for digital research and digital methods for visual research. While it focuses primarily on methods for digital visual research, it also pays specific attention to the settings in which the research may take place or be presented, including artistic and participatory practices. In various chapters, aside from outlining research approaches for studying digital visual materials, we grant importance to the modes of display that matter in visual research, as well as participatory practices that open up the analytical work to experts, whether their knowledge is academic, professional, experiential, or otherwise.

Each chapter (apart from the first) is titled with an adjective and 'images', to characterize a specific outlook for studying digital visual materials. The book starts with the notion of *distant* images, describing methods for analysing large collections of digital images in groups, focusing on their formal patterns and shared visual (and digital) features. It then outlines approaches tailored for studying images in their *networked* context, foregrounding the role of online platforms and digital devices in co-creating meaning. The importance of algorithmic ways of ordering content online is further explored with the chapter dedicated to *critical* images, where we present techniques for studying image bias and how the design of visualizations can be used to critically expose inequalities in the visual representation of different issues online. We then move to discuss *participatory* images, where the focus is on using digital images as starting points for discussion in collaborative settings. Finally, we introduce *machine* images, exploring techniques to study different aspects of generative visual AI, such as their visual bias, content moderation policies and even their potential for participatory endeavours.

As a way of conclusion, we would like to summarize some methodological considerations which we have addressed throughout the book. These are not meant to be exhaustive and should not be taken as a checklist when starting a research project with digital visual methods. Nevertheless, we hope these points of consideration might help to design digital visual research with a careful and reflective perspective, not taking for granted the methods, tools, and formats we illustrate in the book.

No visual research without a (socially relevant) research question

The first important aspect we borrow from digital methods and take to visual research is that research questions always drive the projects. Rather than exploring the affordances and limitations of a particular technology or zooming in on the user demographics of a particular platform, we discuss projects that formulate a question around a social or cultural issue and only later move to data collection (when research questions are further detailed and translated into search terms). Where query design has been developed and matured in the realm of digital methods, we propose to take a similar approach when conducting visual research with generative AI. We, therefore, speak of 'prompt design' instead of the more tech-focused term of 'prompt engineering'.

Furthermore, while we discuss how different tools (including machine vision, software for visual network analysis, and data collection tools) can play a role in such research efforts, we are also sensitive to their flaws and shortcomings. While we employ different tools in the research projects illustrated in the book, the research approach is never tool-driven, and the tool choice always comes after formulating the research question and operationalizing the question into several steps (which may or may not require the use of tools).

Online images are networked

We have worked with two concepts in past research that also have made it into this book: the idea of networked content, and the notion of the folder of images. Strongly connected, they both have impacts on research practices. Networked content and the related approach of networked content analysis take as a point of departure that online content, including online images, is networked by users, platforms, and engines. Therefore, the fact that content is harder to demarcate (as it is less clear where the content ends) calls for digital methods attuned to tracing messages and their resonance online, paying attention to image circulation dynamics. The focus thus turns to the resonance and reappearance of images across online spaces and platforms, and the transformations these images undergo along the way as they become memes, illustrations, fragments, collages, and tropes.

The networked nature of digital images entails considering how users (and platforms) interacting with content online generate collections of linked items. Such collections may be of images posted with the same hashtags or keywords, commented on by users in the same space, or become linked thanks to algorithmic personalization logics of the platforms in which they are embedded. That online images are networked invites researchers to approach images as collections, which can be captured through careful query design, generating folders of images.

Folder of images: looking at images en groupe (while still paying attention to the single image)

The folder of images is not just a metaphor that captures the analytical shift from a single image and its meaning towards the collection of images. The folder also represents a practical moment in the research process. After research questions are formulated, queries or prompts have been designed, a list of sources is compiled, and visual content is located and collected (or generated), researchers often find themselves with a collection of images. This collection may be image files saved in a local or shared folder, spreadsheet, or list with available image URLs. With such a folder of images, the analytical process can start, which often entails them being displayed to facilitate further analysis. While we make the case throughout the book for attending to the collection of images as a unit of analysis, we also maintain how this is often an instrumental moment to access individual images that are further carefully analysed.

Visual formats are not innocent and are context-specific

The proposition we make to approach the study of (and public engagement with) folders of images is to remain as close to the material as possible. Indeed, visual formats (and visual practices) play an essential role in the research approaches we present throughout the book, including, but not limited to, image grids, network graphs, plots, stacks, and catalogues. Building on the argument that visualizations are not innocent but co-produce specific forms of knowledge, we also pay attention to how each display format may support distinct analytical procedures (foreclosing others). For example, when working with small collections of images, it is important to consider that when presenting images side-by-side, they are invited to engage in a conversation. But the question is not just how different arrangements of images may promote various analytical procedures, but also how different visual formats can support participatory actions, design interventions, and multiple forms of engagement with the processes and outcomes of digital visual research.

Data visualization as a way in, not out

In visual and digital research, data visualization is considered a functional tool as part of an elaborate procedure (often outlined in yet another visualization, that of the research protocol). Visualizations can be designed to facilitate analysis, participation, or collaboration. Acknowledging that such visualizations are never neutral and always (somewhat) simplified to make matters legible is important. Here, we can learn from data feminist practices and remember to ask what data or perspective is missing or even actively left out in order to simplify the visual narrative.

It is important to realize that visualizations are a way into further research, not a way out of it. To make sense of the visualizations, one often needs to do a close reading of the images that have been layered, displayed as a grid, or visualized as a network. In other words, visualizations are a means for spending time with the images and a way to connect them with their digital context, including the users that posted them, taking into account the meaning that has been assigned to them on the platform (e.g., by way of captions and hashtags).

What is missing from the folder?

Apart from using visualizations to explore the content of a collection of images, an active research attitude may also involve paying attention to what is not included in the visualization. Who or what is missing from the depiction that a platform offers for a particular issue? These questions are informed by data feminist practices that contribute to digital research and data science through intersectional feminism.

One approach to attending to what is missing in a folder of images connects to the role of social media platforms and search engines in labelling and prioritizing content, thus deciding which images are more visible than others. In this book, we address the topic of inequalities in (visual) data sets, and present techniques for studying bias in the visual representation of various issues online. We discuss successful images and present (visual) research methods aimed at understanding why specific images spread better than others.

In addition, in our chapter on participatory images, we explore the roots of recent (data) feminist theory to learn how 'care and caution' may be integrated into design, digital, and participatory research. In its quest to recognize power imbalances, data feminism attends to multiple perspectives and recognizes the importance of situated and experiential knowledge. Research methods that invite more subjective and personal perspectives on issues may be a good fit for studying societal challenges and debates in participatory settings. In this book, we illustrate how inviting various publics to *talk back to the map* may offer a productive space for joint reflections on matters of concern.

Why visual methods for digital research, now?

What can visual methods for digital research bring to this day and age? In times of war, inequality, and climate crisis, why would we produce a book about the study of images? The question, however valid, is impossible to answer without falling into the traps of credentialling our own work (this is relevant, really!) or oversimplifying the issues or approaches presented in this book. What remains is some space to explain why we needed this book ourselves. We have both conducted digital research (and teaching of digital and visual research methods) on urgent societal topics, including climate change, sustainability, urban nature, and biodiversity. To enable the change necessary to address these issues, be it in policy or on the level of people's behaviour, and the acceptance of such change, we need first to be able to imagine the topic as a matter of concern. Therefore, some of our projects have ventured towards *imagining* a world impacted by climate change (as discussed in chapter 6), while others have focused on collecting online materials about these topics (as discussed in chapters 3 and 4). What have people and organizations already shared to express their views, concerns, and possible countermeasures to climate change or loss of biodiversity in their living environment? These are the kinds of questions and research goals we hope might be explored with the methods discussed in this book.

Final comments

In a networked image-saturated society – in which images link to other images across sources and platforms – methods for visual analysis gain urgency. In addition, with the omnipresence of machine vision (and generation) technologies, digital research needs to account for the variety of visual practices – of human and non-human actors engaging with images online – and the multiple functions online images may have beyond their symbolic power. This book is intended as a guide for researchers and students interested in visual methods, who may consider using them in their research. It offers a range of approaches for *ways of working* with digital images that seek to understand, contextualize, and change perspectives on our digital visual culture, and demonstrates how visual materials can be used to study social and cultural issues.

The approaches we present throughout this book are diverse and heterogeneous. What they have in common is that they all invite visual researchers to remain as close to their objects of study as possible by designing visual methods, visual tools, and visualizations for studying visual materials. In addition, they all foreground the roles that algorithmic tools, including machine vision, can play in such research efforts, always with a critical approach, sensitive to their flaws and shortcomings. We hope this book will provide you with ideas to incorporate visual methods in your research process, or perhaps even design new methodologies for digital visual research.

Notes

1 The poem in *Grosse Fatigue* is by Camille Henrot and Jacob Bromberg, narrated by Ghanaian-American multidisciplinary artist Akwetey Orraca-Tetteh. The music is by French electronic artist and producer Joakim Bouaziz.

2 In the book *Algorithmic Anxiety*, philosopher Patricia de Vries argues that *Grosse Fatigue* repositions Google's search engines from a commercial monopoly to a collection-creation device, which may lead the way out of search engine anxiety (see ch. 4 of De Vries, 2020).

3 A similar 'investigative aesthetics' (Fuller & Weizman, 2021) is also to be found at the centre of various artistic and architectural practices, which, in 'the courtroom and in the gallery', make use of collages and other forms of visual assemblage to engage in investigations into corruption and human rights violations. Among others, the work of research collectives such as Forensic Architecture or Bellingcat is a good example of this approach.

4 In the descriptions and throughout this book, we often speak of 'issues', as we focus on digital image research into social and cultural matters of concern. Of course, these strategies could also be used to study commercial trends or other topics of interest.

5 For a full discussion of networked content analysis, see Niederer (2019).

6 Parts of this chapter have in previous form been published in Bogers et al. (2020).

7 Algorithmic bias is also an emerging topic in the context of (digital) humanities research, where previous work has addressed

the importance of looking at the particular technical set-up of the platforms studied, and has put forward the concept of technicity to address the (socio-)technical specificities of platforms and technologies (Bucher, 2018; Niederer, 2019).

8 For an overview of key texts pertaining to critical research on data sets and algorithms, we recommend the 'Critical Dataset Studies Reading List' (2022), compiled by Frances Corry, Edward B. Kang, Hamsini Sridharan, Sasha Luccioni, Mike Ananny, Kate Crawford: https://knowingmachines.org/reading-list; and the 'Critical Algorithm Studies Reading List' (2016), compiled by Tarleton Gillespie and Nick Seaver: https://socialmediacollective.org /reading-lists/critical-algorithm-studies.

9 For example, ProPublica found that the algorithms used in software that predicts chances of recidivism among convicted criminals (and is relied on by judges across the US) discriminate against people of colour (Spielkamp, 2017). In the Netherlands, the algorithm used to flag fraudulent use of childcare benefits proved discriminatory, causing tremendous financial and social crises for many wrongly accused households (see, for example, the collection of articles on the investigative journalism platform Follow the Money, 2023).

10 User experience designer and design researcher Caroline Sinders proposes three ingredients for incorporating transparency into design practices that make use of machine learning systems. The first ingredient is *legibility*, which she approaches as the 'ability to understand' (Sinders, 2018), which includes designing with words and visuals that allow for publics to understand and read the work and its workings. The second ingredient is *auditability*, which follows from legibility and refers to the 'ability to understand a process, data point or intention, and then understand enough to request changes or give feedback. The third ingredient is *interaction/agency*, as the ability to affect change and/or undertake decision-making from legibility and auditability' (Sinders, 2018). Other responses include the formulation of alternative (design) frameworks, such as 'Design Justice' (Costanza-Chock, 2020) and 'Anti-oppressive Design' (Smyth & Dimond, 2014), and, in response to data science more broadly, data feminism (D'Ignazio & Klein, 2020b; see also chapter 5).

11 The project report of the datasprint in which the initial research took place at a Digital Methods summer school of 2018 can be found at https://digitalmethods.net/Dmi/WinterSchool2018Retraini ngMachine. The paper discussing and contextualizing all methodological considerations and including all parts of this cross-platform and cross-language study can be found in Bogers et al. (2020).

12 These two techniques are discussed in more detail at the end of chapter 3, where we present visual formats for comparing small image collections.

13 In two instances, the man depicted in the images is explicitly violent, pointing a gun at a pregnant belly, or threatening a crying woman with his fist.

14 The project described and depicted here – and in more detail later in the chapter – is that of 'Urban Belonging', in which researchers from Aalborg University, IT University Copenhagen, Gehl, and the Amsterdam University of Applied Sciences collaborated with community partners LGBTQ+ Denmark, Hugs & Food, the Danish Deaf Association, the Danish Disability Association, SIND Denmark, and Mino Denmark, to innovate methods for citizen engagement that foreground diverse and marginalized experiences in urban planning. See also: https://urbanbelonging.com/en.

15 The research for this chapter was done in close collaboration with Carlo De Gaetano, researcher and designer with the Visual Methodologies Collective of the Amsterdam University of Applied Sciences.

16 'After us the deluge', a project by the Visual Methodologies Collective, funded by NWO: www.hva.nl/kc-fdmci/gedeelde-content/projecten /projecten-visual-methodologies/na-ons-de-zondvloed.html.

Bibliography

Agnese, J., Herrera, J., Tao, H. & Zhu, X. (2019, 21 October). *A Survey and Taxonomy of Adversarial Neural Networks for Text-to-Image Synthesis*. arXiv. Retrieved from http://arxiv.org/abs/1910.09399.

Ahmed, S. (2017). The effort to transform: intellectual legacies of Stuart Hall. Retrieved from Feministkilljoys website: https://feministkilljoys .com/2017/05/01/the-effort-to-transform-intellectual-legacies-of -stuart-hall.

Aiello, G. (2016, 28 April). Taking stock. Retrieved from Ethnography Matters website: https://ethnographymatters.net/blog/2016/04/28 /taking-stock.

Aiello, G., Atabaki, A., Bardelli, F., Borra, E., Bosma, J., Eleftheriadou, A., Garceau, A., Gorter, E., van Kollenburg, D., Lueke, K., Ricci, D., van Rosmalen, L., Salazar, G., Sommers, A., Verlouw, C. & Zwaan, A. (2016). A critical genealogy of the Getty Images Lean In Collection. Retrieved from Digital Methods Initiative website: https://digitalmethods.net/Dmi/WinterSchool2016CriticalGenealogy GettyImagesLeanIn.

Aiello, G. & Parry, K. (2020). *Visual Communication: Understanding Images in Media Culture*. London: SAGE Publications.

Aiello, G. & Woodhouse, A. (2016). When corporations come to define the visual politics of gender: the case of Getty Images. *Journal of Language and Politics*, 15(3), 352–68: doi.org/ 10.1075/ jlp.15.3.08aie.

Allen, J. (2020). Beyond the media reveal: if we sought to go beyond the media reveal, what new practices of knowledge should emerge? *Seismograf*: doi.org/10.48233/SEISMOGRAF2504.

Anderson, C. W., Kennedy, H. & Aiello, G. (n.d.). Generic visuals in the news: the role of stock photos and simple data visualizations in assembling publics. Retrieved from https://genericvisuals.leeds.ac.uk.

Baccarne, B., Briones, M. de los Á., Baack, S., Maemura, E., Omena, J. J., Zhou, P., & Ferreira, H. (2015). Does love win? The mechanics of memetics. Retrieved from Digital Methods Initiative website: https://wiki.digitalmethods.net/Dmi/SummerSchool2015DoesLoveWin.

Baio, A. (2022, 30 August). Exploring 12 million of the 2.3 billion images used to train Stable Diffusion's image generator. Retrieved from Waxy.org website: https://waxy.org/2022/08/exploring-12-million-of-the-images-used-to-train-stable-diffusions-image-generator.

Ballvé, T. (2012). The new aesthetic part I: seeing like a machine. Territorial Masquerades. Retrieved from https://territorialmasquerades.net/the-new-aesthetic-part-i-seeing-like-a-machine.

Banham, R. (1969). *The Architecture of the Well-Tempered Environment.* Oxford: Architectural Press.

Banks, M. (2018). *Using Visual Data in Qualitative Research.* London: SAGE Publications: doi.org/ 10.4135/9781526445933.

Bano, M. (2018). Artificial intelligence is demonstrating gender bias – and it's our fault. Retrieved from King's College London website: www.kcl.ac.uk/news/artificial-intelligence-is-demonstrating-gender-bias-and-its-our-fault.

Beaumont, R. (2022, 31 March). LAION-5B: a new era of open large-scale multi-modal datasets. LAION. Retrieved from https://laion.ai/blog/laion-5b.

Becher, B. & Becher, H. (2004). *Typologies of Industrial Buildings.* Cambridge, MA: MIT Press.

Bell, P. (2004). Content analysis of visual images. In T. Van Leeuwen & C. Jewitt (eds.), *The Handbook of Visual Analysis* (pp. 10–34). London: SAGE Publications: doi.org/10.4135/9780857020062.n2.

Benkler, Y., Faris, R. & Roberts, H. (2018). *Network Propaganda: Manipulation, Disinformation, and Radicalization in American Politics.* New York: Oxford University Press.

Bianchi, F., Kalluri, P., Durmus, E., Ladhak, F., Cheng, M., Nozza, D., Hashimoto, T., Jurafsky, D., Zou, J. & Caliskan, A. (2022, 7 November). *Easily Accessible Text-to-Image Generation Amplifies Demographic Stereotypes at Large Scale.* arXiv. Retrieved from http://arxiv.org/abs/2211.03759.

Birhane, A., Prabhu, V. U. & Kahembwe, E. (2021, 5 October). *Multimodal Datasets: Misogyny, Pornography, and Malignant Stereotypes.* arXiv: doi.org/10.48550/arXiv.2110.01963.

Bogers, L., Niederer, S., Bardelli, F. & De Gaetano, C. (2020). Confronting bias in the online representation of pregnancy. *Convergence: The*

International Journal of Research into New Media Technologies, 26(5–6), 1037–59: doi.org/10.1177/1354856520938606.

Borra, E. (2023). *Object-Activity: Repurposing the Dual Nature of Web Data for Digital Research*. University of Amsterdam. Retrieved from https://dare.uva.nl/search?identifier=20d48011-aa50-46d1-936d-09a8b6b921f9.

Borra, E. & Rieder, B. (2014). Programmed method: developing a toolset for capturing and analyzing tweets. *Aslib Journal of Information Management*, 66(3), 262–78: doi.org/10.1108/AJIM-09-2013-0094.

Borra, E., Weltevrede, E., Ciuccarelli, P., Kaltenbrunner, A., Laniado, D., Magni, G., Mauri, M., Rogers, R. & Venturini, T. (2015). Societal controversies in Wikipedia articles. In *Proceedings of the 33rd Annual ACM Conference on Human Factors in Computing Systems* (pp. 193–6). Seoul Republic of Korea: ACM: https://doi.org/10.1145/2702123.2702436.

Bounegru, L., Gray, J., Colombo, G., Tegegne, Y. & Tsubaki, R. (2022). *Out of the Flames: Mapping Online Engagement and Public Narratives around the 2019 Amazon Rainforest Fires*: doi.org/10.13140/RG.2.2.11633.56164.

Bounegru, L., Gray, J., Venturini, T. & Mauri, M. (2018). *A Field Guide to 'Fake News' and Other Information Disorders: A Collection of Recipes for Those Who Love to Cook with Digital Methods*. Amsterdam: Public Data Lab. Retrieved from https://dx.doi.org/10.2139/ssrn.3097666.

boyd, d. & Crawford, K. (2011). Six provocations for Big Data. *SSRN Electronic Journal*: doi.org/10.2139/ssrn.1926431.

Bridle, J. (director). (2018). Artificial Intelligence is not neutral. Online video interview, retrieved from www.youtube.com/watch?v=zDHSD4twyIA.

Bridle, J. (2023, 16 March). The stupidity of AI. *The Guardian*. Retrieved from www.theguardian.com/technology/2023/mar/16/the-stupidity-of-ai-artificial-intelligence-dall-e-chatgpt.

Bucher, T. (2018). *If … Then: Algorithmic Power and Politics*. Oxford University Press: doi.org/10.1093/oso/9780190493028.001.0001.

Bucher, T. & Helmond, A. (2018). The affordances of social media platforms. In J. Burgess, A. Marwick & T. Poell (eds.), *The SAGE Handbook of Social Media* (pp. 233–53). SAGE Publications.

Buolamwini, J. & Gebru, T. (2018). Gender shades: intersectional accuracy disparities in commercial gender classification. In S. A. Friedler & C. Wilson (eds.), *Proceedings of the 1st Conference on Fairness, Accountability and Transparency* (pp. 77–91). Proceedings of Machine Learning Research. Retrieved from https://proceedings.mlr.press/v81/buolamwini18a.html.

Burgos-Thorsen, S. (2023). *Expanding Data Imaginaries in Urban Planning: Foregrounding Lived Experience and Community Voices in Studies of Cities with Participatory and Digital Visual Methods.* Aalborg Universitetsforlag: https://doi.org/10.54337/aau550446611.

Calvillo González, N. & Mesa del Castillo, M. (2018). Tender infrastructures: designing with care, or contributions to 'matters of care' in architecture. *Revista Diseña*, 12, 172–95: doi.org/ 10.7764/ disena.12.172-195.

Carter, S., Armstrong, Z., Schubert, L., Johnson, I. & Olah, C. (2019). Exploring neural networks with activation atlases. *Distill*, 4(3): doi .org/10.23915/distill.00015.

Cattaneo, A., Hu, Y., Macrini, L., Moreschi, N., Puca, L., Sghirinzetti, S., & Zheng, C. (2023). Eye to AI – exposing human biases on climate change through AI. Retrieved from from DensityDesign Research Lab website: https://densitydesign.github.io/dd18-g06 /index.html.

Chou, J., Murillo, O. & Ibars, R. (2017). How to recognize exclusion in AI. Retrieved from Microsoft Design website: https://medium.com /microsoft-design/how-to-recognize-exclusion-in-ai-ec2d6d89f850.

Chun, W. H. K. (2018). Queerying homophily. In C. Apprich, W. H. K. Chun, F. Cramer, & H. Steyerl, eds., *Pattern Discrimination* (pp. 59–97). Lüneburg: meson press, University of Minnesota Press; 59-97: doi.org/10.25969/MEDIAREP/12350.

Ciston, S. (2022). A critical fieldguide for working with machine learning datasets. Retrieved from Knowing Machines website: https://knowingmachines.org/critical-field-guide.

Cole, S. (2022, 24 August). This AI tool is being used to make freaky, machine-generated porn. Retrieved from Vice website: www .vice.com/en/article/xgygy4/stable-diffusion-stability-ai-nsfw-ai -generated-porn.

Collins, P. H. (1990). Black feminist thought in the matrix of domination. *Black Feminist Thought: Knowledge, Consciousness, and the Politics of Empowerment*, 138(1990), 221–38.

Colombo, G. (2018). The design of composite images (doctoral dissertation). Politecnico di Milano. Retrieved from http://hdl.handle.net /10589/141266.

Colombo, G. (2019). Studying digital images in groups: The folder of images. In I. Mariani & L. Rampino (eds.), *Advancements in Design Research: 11 PhD Theses on Design as We Do in Polimi*. Milan: Angeli Open Access. Retrieved from https:// library.oapen.org/bitstream/handle/20.500.12657/24725/376-99Z _Book%20Manuscript-1749-1-10-20190211.pdf?sequence=1 #page=186.

Colombo, G. & Azzi, M. (2016, 22 July). Fakes, flames and memes [part 1]. Retrieved from DensityDesign Research Lab website: https://medium.com/densitydesign/fakes-flames-and-memes-part -1-9707961b7b10.

Colombo, G., Bounegru, L. & Gray, J. (2023). Visual models for social media image analysis: groupings, engagement, trends, and rankings. *International Journal of Communication*, 17, 28.

Colombo, G. & De Gaetano, C. (2020). Dutch political Instagram: junk news, follower ecologies and artificial amplification. In R. Rogers & S. Niederer (eds.), *The Politics of Social Media Manipulation* (pp. 147–68). Amsterdam University Press: doi.org/10 .1515/9789048551675-006.

Colombo, G., De Gaetano, C. & Niederer, S. (2023). Prompting for biodiversity: visual research with generative AI. Retrieved from Digital Methods Initiative website: https://wiki.digitalmethods.net /Dmi/PromptingForBiodiversity.

Colombo, G. & Niederer, S. (2021). Diseña 19: visual methods for online images – collection, circulation, and machine co-creation. *Diseña*, 19, 7: doi.org/https://doi.org/10.7764/disena.19.Intro.

Costanza-Chock, S. (2020). *Design Justice: Community-Led Practices to Build the Worlds We Need*. Cambridge, MA: MIT Press.

Crawford, K. & Joler, V. (2018). Anatomy of an AI system: the Amazon Echo as an anatomical map of human labor, data and planetary resources. AI Now Institute and Share Lab: https://anatomyof.ai.

Crawford, K. & Paglen, T. (2019). Excavating AI: the politics of images in machine learning training sets. Retrieved from https://excavating.ai.

D'Andréa, C. & Mints, A. (2019). Studying the live cross-platform circulation of images with computer vision API: an experiment based on a sports media event. *International Journal of Communication*, 13, 21.

D'Andréa, C, & Mints, A. (2021). Investigating cross-platform visual issuefication: the case of Brazil's Pantanal wildfires. Retrieved from #SMARTDataSprint website: https://smart.inovamedialab.org /editions/2021-platformisation/project-reports/investigating-cross -platform.

De Gaetano, C., Niederer, S., Pearce, W. & Sánchez Querubín, N. (2022). What should climate change look like? Mapping climate imaginaries across eco-fiction genres and platforms. Retrieved from www.digitalmethods.net/Dmi/ClimateImaginaries.

De Geuzen (2006). Global anxiety monitor. Retrieved from www .geuzen.org/anxiety.

De Vries, P. (2020). *Algorithmic Anxiety in Contemporary Art: A Kierkegaardian Inquiry into the Imaginary of Possibility*. Amsterdam: Institute of Network Cultures. Retrieved from https://networkcultures.org/wp-content/uploads/2020/06 /AlgorithmicAnxietyPDF.pdf.

DelSignore, P. (2023, 5 April). Midjourney's crazy new Describe feature. Retrieved from The Generator website: https://medium.com/the-generator/midjourneys-crazy-new-describe-feature-a96cc09203cc.

Denson, S. (2020). *Discorrelated Images*. Durham: Duke University Press.

D'Ignazio, C. & Klein, L. F. (2016). Feminist data visualization. Retrieved from www.kanarinka.com/wp-content/uploads/2015/07/IEEE_Feminist_Data_Visualization.pdf.

D'Ignazio, C. & Klein, L. F. (2020a). Seven intersectional feminist principles for equitable and actionable COVID-19 data. *Big Data & Society*, 7(2): https://doi.org/10.1177/2053951720942544.

D'Ignazio, C. & Klein, L. F. (2020b). *Data Feminism*. Cambridge, MA: MIT Press.

D'Ignazio, C., Klein, L. & Livio, M. (2021). Feminist data practices: conversations with Catherine D'Ignazio, Lauren Klein, and Maya Livio (interviewers: S. Niederer & G. Colombo). Retrieved from http://ojs.uc.cl/index.php/Disena/article/view/41545.

Dijkstra, L. J. & Krieg, L. J. (2016). From MDMA to Lady Gaga: expertise and contribution behavior of editing communities on Wikipedia. *Procedia Computer Science*, 101, 96–106: doi.org/10.1016/j.procs.2016.11.013.

DiSalvo, C. (2009). Design and the construction of publics. *Design Issues*, 25(1), 48–63: doi.org/10.1162/desi.2009.25.1.48.

Domestic Data Streamers (2022, October). Prompt book for data lovers II ♥. Retrieved from https://docs.google.com/presentation/d/1V8d6TIlKqB1j5xPFH7cCmgKOV_fMs4Cb4dwgjD5GIsg.

Drucker, J. (2014). *Graphesis: Visual Forms of Knowledge Production*. Cambridge, MA: Harvard University Press.

Eco, U. (2009). *The Infinity of Lists*. New York: Rizzoli.

e-flux (2017). Forensic Architecture: towards an investigative aesthetics – announcements. Retrieved from www.e-flux.com/announcements/93328/forensic-architecturetowards-an-investigative-aesthetics.

Ekenstam, L. (2023a, 2 February). The lazy prompt to knolling is simple [Item]+[Type]+Knolling https://t.co/B15hRCjg6N. Twitter. Retrieved from Twitter website: https://twitter.com/LinusEkenstam/status/1620936510416764929.

Ekenstam, L. (2023b, 13 March). Tutorial: dynamic prompting [Substack newsletter]. Retrieved from Inside My Head website: https://linusekenstam.substack.com/p/tutorial-dynamic-prompting.

Engelhardt, Y., Waller, R., Frascara, J., Van der Waarde, K., Garrett, M., Schriver, K., … Požar, C. (2016). *On Information Design*. Ljubljana: The Museum of Architecture and Design – Društvo Pekinpah. Retrieved from www.dlib.si/stream/URN:NBN:SI:doc-2N1R3N8A/8475a930-3883-43a1-b3d0-2a97bca66fea/PDF.

Farías, I. & Bender, T. (2010). *Urban Assemblages: How Actor–Network Theory Changes Urban Studies*. London: Routledge.

Farocki, H. (2004). Phantom images. *Public*, 29. Retrieved from https://public.journals.yorku.ca/index.php/public/article/view/30354.

Fehrmann, G., Linz, E., Schumacher, E. & Weingart, B. (eds.) (2004). *Originalkopie. Praktiken des Sekundären*. Retrieved from https://kups.ub.uni-koeln.de/2378.

Feldman, E. (2023, 24 January). Are A.I. image generators violating copyright laws? Retrieved from *Smithsonian Magazine* website: www.smithsonianmag.com/smart-news/are-ai-image-generators-stealing-from-artists-180981488.

Follow the Money (2022). Toeslagenaffaire. Retrieved from Follow the Money – Platform voor onderzoeksjournalistiek website: www.ftm.nl/tag/toeslagenaffaire.

FOMU (2017). BRAAKLAND: Coralie Vogelaar – recognized / not recognized. Retrieved from www.braakland-fomu.be/vogelaar.php.

Frosh, P. (2013). Beyond the image bank. Digital commercial photography. In M. Lister (ed.), *The Photographic Image in Digital Culture* (2nd edition, pp. 131–48). London, New York: Routledge, Taylor & Francis Group.

Fuller, M. & Weizman, E. (2021). *Investigative Aesthetics: Conflicts and Commons in the Politics of Truth*. London, New York: Verso.

Future of Life Institute (2023, 22 March). Pause giant AI experiments: an open letter. Retrieved from Future of Life Institute website: https://futureoflife.org/open-letter/pause-giant-ai-experiments.

Gault, M. (2022, 31 August). An AI-Generated artwork won first place at a state fair fine arts competition, and artists are pissed. Retrieved from Vice website: www.vice.com/en/article/bvmvqm/an-ai-generated-artwork-won-first-place-at-a-state-fair-fine-arts-competition-and-artists-are-pissed.

Gavves, E., Snoek, C. G. M. & Smeulders, A. W. M. (2012). Visual synonyms for landmark image retrieval. *Computer Vision and Image Understanding*, 116(2), 238–49: doi.org/10.1016/j.cviu.2011.10.004.

Geboers, M. (2019). 'Writing' oneself into tragedy: visual user practices and spectatorship of the Alan Kurdi images on Instagram. *Visual Communication*: https://doiorg/10.1177/1470357219857118.

Geboers, M. (2022). The social visuality of distant suffering: how social media create new boundaries of visibility (doctoral dissertation). University of Amsterdam.

Geboers, M., Stolero, N., Scuttari, A., van Vliet, L. & Ridley, A. (2020). Why buttons matter: repurposing Facebook's reactions for analysis of the social visual. *International Journal of Communication*, 14, 22.

Geboers, M. A. & Van De Wiele, C. T. (2020). Machine vision and social media images: why hashtags matter. *Social Media + Society*, 6(2): https://doi.org/10.1177/2056305120928485.

Generic Visuals in the News Team (2022). The role of generic visuals in assembling publics in the news. Retrieved from Digital Methods Initiative website: https://wiki.digitalmethods.net/Dmi/SummerSchool2022GenericVisuals.

Gerlitz, C. & Helmond, A. (2013). The like economy: social buttons and the data-intensive web. *New Media & Society*, 15(8), 1348–65: https://doi.org/10.1177/1461444812472322.

Gibbs, M., Meese, J., Arnold, M., Nansen, B. & Carter, M. (2015). #Funeral and Instagram: death, social media, and platform vernacular. *Information, Communication & Society*, 18(3), 255–68: https://doi.org/10.1080/1369118X.2014.987152.

Golby, J. (2023, 27 March). I thought I was immune to being fooled online. Then I saw the pope in a coat. *The Guardian*. Retrieved from www.theguardian.com/commentisfree/2023/mar/27/pope-coat-ai-image-baby-boomers.

Grønstad, A. & Vågnes, Ø. (2006). An interview with W. J. T. Mitchell. *Image & Narrative*, 15: Battles around images: iconoclasm and beyond. Retrieved from www.imageandnarrative.be/inarchive/iconoclasm/gronstad_vagnes.htm.

Gurfinkel, J. (2023, 28 March). AI and the American smile. Retrieved from Medium website: https://medium.com/@socialcreature/ai-and-the-american-smile-76d23a0fbfaf.

Hand, M. (2017). Visuality in social media: researching images, circulations and practices. In L. Sloan & A. Quan-Haase (eds.), *The SAGE Handbook of Social Media Research Methods* (pp. 215–32). London: SAGE Publications.

Hand, M. (2020). Photography meets social media: image making and sharing in a continually networked present. In *The Handbook of Photography Studies* (p. 17). London: Routledge.

Haraway, D. (1988). Situated knowledges: the science question in feminism and the privilege of partial perspective. *Feminist Studies*, 14(3), 575–99: https://doi.org/10.2307/3178066.

Harrison, M. (2023, 8 February). ChatGPT is just an automated mansplaining machine. Retrieved from Futurism website: https://futurism.com/artificial-intelligence-automated-mansplaining-machine.

Harvey, P., Reeves, M. & Ruppert, E. (2013). ANTICIPATING FAILURE: transparency devices and their effects. *Journal of Cultural Economy*, 6(3), 294–312: https://doi.org/10.1080/17530350.2012.739973.

Henrot, C. (2017). An interview with French artist Camille Henrot. *CRASH Magazine* (interviewers: C. Cosson & E. Luciani). Retrieved from www.crash.fr/an-interview-with-french-artist-camille-henrot.

Hern, A. (2020, 21 September). Twitter apologises for 'racist' image-cropping algorithm. *The Guardian*. Retrieved from www.theguardian.com/technology/2020/sep/21/twitter-apologises-for-racist-image-cropping-algorithm.

Hern, A. & Bhuiyan, J. (2023, 14 March). OpenAI says new model GPT-4 is more creative and less likely to invent facts. *The Guardian*. Retrieved from www.theguardian.com/technology/2023/mar/14/chat-gpt-4-new-model.

Herring, S. (2010). Web content analysis: expanding the paradigm. In J. Hunsinger, L. Klastrup & M. Allen (eds.), *International Handbook of Internet Research* (pp. 233–49). Dordrecht: Springer.

Herrman, J. (2016, 24 August). Inside Facebook's (totally insane, unintentionally gigantic, hyperpartisan) political-media machine. *The New York Times*. Retrieved from www.nytimes.com/2016/08/28/magazine/inside-facebooks-totally-insane-unintentionally-gigantic-hyperpartisan-political-media-machine.html.

Hill, S. (n.d.). Pinterest board: drawing prompts. Retrieved from Pinterest website: www.pinterest.it/samariah84/drawing-prompts.

Hochman, N., Manovich, L. & Chow, J. (2013). Phototrails. Retrieved from http://phototrails.info/visualizations/photoplot-visualization.

Hochschild, A. R. (1983). *The Managed Heart: Commercialisation of Human Feeling*. Berkeley: University of California Press.

Hoelzl, I. & Marie, R. (2015). *Softimage: Towards a New Theory of the Digital Image*. Bristol: Intellect.

Hu, Y., Manikonda, L. & Kambhampati, S. (2014). What we Instagram: a first analysis of Instagram photo content and user types. In *Proceedings of the International AAAI Conference on Web and Social Media*, 8(1), 595–8.

Jenkins, H. (2006). *Convergence Culture: Where Old and New Media Collide*. New York University Press.

Jina AI GmbH (2023). PromptPerfect – elevate your prompts to perfection. Retrieved from https://promptperfect.jina.ai.

Ju, W., Oehlberg, L., Follmer, S., Fox, S. & Kuznetsov, S. (2021). *Search Atlas: Visualizing Divergent Search Results across Geopolitical Borders*. New York: Association for Computing Machinery. Retrieved from https://hdl.handle.net/1721.1/145963.

Jurgenson, N. (2019). *The Social Photo: On Photography and Social Media*. New York: Verso Books.

Karpathy, A. (2014). T-SNE visualization of CNN codes. Retrieved from https://cs.stanford.edu/people/karpathy/cnnembed.

Karsgaard, C. & MacDonald, M. (2020). Picturing the pipeline: mapping settler colonialism on Instagram. *New Media & Society*, 22(7), 1206–26: https://doi.org/10.1177/1461444820912541.

Kelty, C. M. (2019). *The Participant: A Century of Participation in Four Stories*. Chicago, London: The University of Chicago Press.

Klippenstein, K. (2023, 25 July). As actors strike for AI protections, Netflix lists $900,000 AI job. Retrieved 2 August 2023, from The Intercept website: https://theintercept.com/2023/07/25/strike -hollywood-ai-disney-netflix.

Koch, B., Denton, E., Hanna, A. & Foster, J. G. (2021, 3 December). *Reduced, Reused and Recycled: The Life of a Dataset in Machine Learning Research.* arXiv. Retrieved from http://arxiv.org/abs/2112 .01716.

Krippendorff, K. (2018). *Content Analysis: An Introduction to Its Methodology.* London: SAGE Publications.

Kumar, S., Coggins, G., McMonagle, S., Schlögl, S., Liao, H.-T., Stevenson, M., Bardelli, F. & Ben-David, A. (2013). Cross-lingual art spaces on Wikipedia. Digital Methods Initiative. Retrieved from Digital Methods Initiative website: https://digitalmethods.net/Dmi /CrossLingualArtSpacesOnWikipedia.

Lambrecht, A. & Tucker, C. E. (2020, 12 April). Apparent algorithmic discrimination and real-time algorithmic learning in digital search advertising [SSRN Scholarly Paper]. Rochester, NY: doi.org/10.2139 /ssrn.3570076.

Latour, B. (2005). *Reassembling the Social: An Introduction to Actor-Network-Theory.* Oxford University Press.

Latour, B., Jensen, P., Venturini, T., Grauwin, S. & Boullier, D. (2012). 'The whole is always smaller than its parts' – a digital test of Gabriel Tardes' monads. *The British Journal of Sociology*, 63(4), 590–615: https://doi.org/10.1111/j.1468-4446.2012.01428.x.

Leaver, T., Highfield, T. & Abidin, C. (2020). *Instagram: Visual Social Media Cultures.* Cambridge, UK and Medford, MA: Polity.

Lexica (2023). Lexica – search query: 'nazi'. Retrieved from Lexica website: https://lexica.art/?q=nazi.

Lister, M. (ed.). (2013). *The Photographic Image in Digital Culture* (2nd edition). London, New York: Routledge, Taylor & Francis Group.

Liu, G. (2022, 21 June). DALL-E 2 made its first magazine cover. Retrieved from *Cosmopolitan* website: www.cosmopolitan.com /lifestyle/a40314356/dall-e-2-artificial-intelligence-cover.

Lorusso, S. (2015). Reblogs or context is the new content [digital image, video, website]. Retrieved from https://silviolorusso.com /work/reblogs-or-context-is-the-new-content.

Luccioni, S. (2022). Diffusion bias explorer – a Hugging Face space by society-ethics. Retrieved from Hugging Face website: https:// huggingface.co/spaces/society-ethics/DiffusionBiasExplorer.

Madani, D. (2019). Raging rainforest fires darken skies in Brazil, inspire #prayforamazonia. *NBC News.* Retrieved from www .nbcnews.com/news/world/amazon-fires-2019-deforestation-hashtag -prayforamazonia-n1044976.

Madsen, A. K., Burgos-Thorsen, S., De Gaetano, C., Ehn, D., Groen, M., Niederer, S., ... Simonsen, T. (2023). The urban belonging photo app: a toolkit for studying place attachments with digital and participatory methods. *Methodological Innovations*: https://doi.org /10.1177/20597991231185351.

Mannay, D. (2016). *Visual, Narrative and Creative Research Methods: Application, Reflection and Ethics*. London: Routledge, Taylor & Francis Group.

Manovich, L. (2010). Rise of 'compositions' (vs. 'portraits') in covers of Time magazine, 1923–1989 as a timeline. Retrieved from www.flickr .com/photos/culturevis/4347477551/in/set-72157623414034532.

Manovich, L. (2011a). 776 van Gogh paintings (1881–1890). Retrieved from www.flickr.com/photos/culturevis/5910819865/in/album -72157627135422710.

Manovich, L. (2011b). What is visualisation? *Visual Studies*, 26(1), 36–49: https://doi.org/10.1080/1472586X.2011.548488.

Manovich, L. (2011c). Style space: how to compare image sets and follow their evolution. Retrieved from http://manovich.net/content /04-projects/073-style-space/70_article_2011.pdf.

Manovich, L. (2017). *Instagram and Contemporary Image*. Self-published.

Manovich, L. (2019). *AI Aesthetics*. Moscow: Strelka Press.

Manovich, L. (2020). *Cultural Analytics*. Cambridge, MA: MIT Press.

Manzini, E. (2015). *Design, When Everybody Designs: An Introduction to Design for Social Innovation*. Cambridge, MA: MIT Press.

Marres, N. (2012). The redistribution of methods: on intervention in digital social research, broadly conceived. *The Sociological Review*, 60(1 – suppl.), 139–65: doi.org/10.1111/j.1467-954X.2012.02121.x.

Marres, N. (2015a). *Material Participation: Technology, the Environment, and Everyday Publics* (paperback edition). New York: Palgrave Macmillan.

Marres, N. (2015b). Why map issues? On controversy analysis as a digital method. *Science, Technology, & Human Values*, 40(5), 655–86: https://doi.org/10.1177/0162243915574602.

Marres, N., Colombo, G., Bounegru, L., Gray, J., Gerlitz, C. & Tripp, J. (2023). Testing and not testing for coronavirus on Twitter: surfacing testing situations across scales with interpretative methods. *Social Media + Society*, 9(3): https://doi.org/10.1177 /20563051231196538.

Marres, N. & Gerlitz, C. (2016). Interface methods: renegotiating relations between digital social research, STS and sociology. *The Sociological Review*, 64(1), 21–46: https://doi.org/10.1111/1467 -954X.12314.

Mauri, M., Elli, T., Caviglia, G., Uboldi, G. & Azzi, M. (2017). RAWGraphs: a visualisation platform to create open outputs. In *Proceedings of the 12th Biannual Conference on Italian SIGCHI Chapter*, 1–5. Cagliari: ACM: https://doi.org/10.1145/3125571 .3125585.

McMillan, S. J. (2000). The microscope and the moving target: the challenge of applying content analysis to the World Wide Web. *Journalism & Mass Communication Quarterly*, 77(1), 80–98.

Media Manipulation Casebook (2020). Evidence collages. Retrieved from Media Manipulation Casebook website: https://mediamanipulation .org/definitions/evidence-collages.

Menkman, R. (2009). *Glitch Studies Manifesto*. Self-published.

Menkman, R. (2011). *The Glitch Moment(um)*. Amsterdam: Institute of Network Cultures.

Meunier, A., Gray, J. & Ricci, D. (2021, 16 December). A New AI Lexicon: algorithm trouble. Retrieved from A New AI Lexicon website: https://medium.com/a-new-ai-lexicon/a-new-ai-lexicon -algorithm-trouble-50312d985216.

Midjourney (2022). Midjourney community guidelines. Retrieved from https://docs.midjourney.com/docs/community-guidelines.

Miller, C. (2017). From sex object to gritty woman: the evolution of women in stock photos. *The New York Times*. Retrieved from www .nytimes.com/2017/09/07/upshot/from-sex-object-to-gritty-woman -the-evolution-of-women-in-stock-photos.html.

Mitchell, W. J. T. (1992). The pictorial turn. *Artforum*, 30(7). Retrieved from www.artforum.com/print/199203/the-pictorial-turn-33613.

Mitchell, W. J. T. (1994). *Picture Theory: Essays on Verbal and Visual Representation* (paperback edition). University of Chicago Press.

Moholy-Nagy, L. (1947). *Vision in Motion*. Chicago: Institute of Design.

Monge, J. C. (2022, 25 August). DALL-E2 vs Stable Diffusion: same prompt, different results. Retrieved from MLearning.ai website: https://medium.com/mlearning-ai/dall-e2-vs-stable-diffusion-same -prompt-different-results-e795c84adc56.

Mordvintsev, A., Olah, C. & Tyka, M. (2015, 8 July). DeepDream – a code example for visualizing neural networks. Retrieved from https://web.archive.org/web/20150708233542/http://googleresearch .blogspot.co.uk/2015/07/deepdream-code-example-for-visualizing .html.

Moretti, F. (2013). *Distant Reading*. London, New York: Verso.

Mosseri, A. (2021). Shedding more light on how Instagram works. Retrieved from Instagram website: https://about.instagram.com/blog /announcements/shedding-more-light-on-how-instagram-works.

Munk, A. K., Meunier, A. & Venturini, T. (2019). Data sprints: a collaborative format in digital controversy mapping. In J. Vertesi,

D. Ribes, C. DiSalvo, Y. Loukissas, L. Forlano, D. K. Rosner, ... H. R. Shell (eds.), *digitalSTS* (pp. 472–96). Princeton University Press. JSTOR: doi.org/10.2307/j.ctvc77mp9.34.

Neal, D. M. (2010). Emotion-based tags in photographic documents: the interplay of text, image, and social influence / Les étiquettes basées sur des émotions dans les documents photographiques: l'interaction entre le texte, l'image et l'influence sociale. *Canadian Journal of Information and Library Science*, 34(3), 329–53: doi.org/10.1353/ils.2010.0000.

Nešović, D. (2022a). No shot like screenshot: banal, sublime and dangerous. Retrieved from Institute of Network Cultures website: https://networkcultures.org/longform/2022/01/19/no-shot-like-screenshot-banal-sublime-and-dangerous.

Nešović, D. (2022b). *The Lazy Art of Screenshot*. Amsterdam: Institute of Network Cultures.

New Knowledge (2018). 'The tactics & tropes of the Internet Research Agency'. White Paper. Austin, TX: New Knowledge: https://disinformationreport.blob.core.windows.net/disinformation-report/NewKnowledge-DisinformationReport-Whitepaper.pdf.

New Oxford American Dictionary (2023). Prompt (noun). Oxford University Press.

Nicoletti, L. & Bass, D. (2023, 23 April). Humans are biased. Generative AI is even worse. Bloomberg.Com. Retrieved from www.bloomberg.com/graphics/2023-generative-ai-bias.

Niederer, S. (2018). *Networked Images: Visual Methodologies for the Digital Age*. Amsterdam University of Applied Sciences.

Niederer, S. (2019). *Networked Content Analysis: The Case of Climate Change*. Amsterdam: Institute of Network Cultures.

Niederer, S. & Colombo, G. (2019). Visual methodologies for networked images: designing visualizations for collaborative research, cross-platform analysis, and public participation. *Revista Diseña*, 14, 40–67: doi.org/10.7764/disena.14.40-67.

Niederer, S. & Colombo, G. (2023). The earnest platform: U.S. presidential candidates, COVID-19, and social issues on Instagram. In R. Rogers (ed.), *The Propagation of Misinformation in Social Media: A Cross-Platform Analysis* (pp. 139–64). Amsterdam University Press: doi.org/10.2307/jj.1231864.

Niederer, S. & van Dijck, J. (2010). Wisdom of the crowd or technicity of content? Wikipedia as a sociotechnical system. *New Media & Society*, 12(8), 1368–87: https://doi.org/10.1177/1461444810365297.

Nielsen, L. (2023, 18 April). An advanced guide to writing prompts for Midjourney (text-to-image). Retrieved from MLearning.ai website: https://medium.com/mlearning-ai/an-advanced-guide-to-writing-prompts-for-midjourney-text-to-image-aa12a1e33b6.

Noble, S. U. (2018). *Algorithms of Oppression: How Search Engines Reinforce Racism*. New York University Press.

Ochigame, R. & Ye, K. (2021). Search atlas: visualizing divergent search results across geopolitical borders. In *DIS '21: Proceedings of the 2021 ACM Designing Interactive Systems Conference* (pp. 1970–83). Virtual Event USA: Association for Computing Machinery, New York: https://doi.org/10.1145/3461778.3462032.

Odell, J. (2015). Peripheral landscapes: people, gods, and flora/fauna. Retrieved from www.jennyodell.com/peripheral-landscapes.html.

Omena, J. J., Pilipets, E., Gobbo, B. & Chao, J. (2021). The potentials of Google Vision API-based networks to study natively digital images. *Revista Diseña*, 19: doi.org/10.7764/disena.19.Article.1.

Omena, J. J., Rabello, E. T. & Mintz, A. G. (2020). Digital methods for hashtag engagement research. *Social Media + Society*, 6(3): doi.org/10.1177/2056305120940697.

O'Neil, C. (2016). *Weapons of Math Destruction: How Big Data Increases Inequality and Threatens Democracy*. Harmondsworth: Penguin UK.

Open Art (2022). Stable Diffusion prompt book. Retrieved from https://openart.ai/promptbook.

OpenAI (2021, 5 January). DALL·E: creating images from text. Retrieved from https://openai.com/research/dall-e.

OpenAI (2022a, April). DALL·E 2 preview – risks and limitations. Retrieved from https://github.com/openai/dalle-2-preview/blob/eeec5a1843b1d17cb9ed113117a2fcaa9206a564/system-card.md.

OpenAI (2022b,18 July). Reducing bias and improving safety in DALL·E 2. Retrieved from OpenAI blog website: https://openai.com/blog/reducing-bias-and-improving-safety-in-dall-e-2.

OpenAI (2022c, 19 September). DALL·E – content policy. Retrieved from https://labs.openai.com.

Paglen, T. (2016). Invisible images (your pictures are looking at you). Retrieved from The New Inquiry website: https://thenewinquiry.com/invisible-images-your-pictures-are-looking-at-you.

Papacharissi, Z. (2014). *Affective Publics: Sentiment, Technology, and Politics*. New York: Oxford University Press.

Parry, K. (2023). *A Theory of Assembly: From Museums to Memes*. Minneapolis: University of Minnesota Press.

Pearce, W. & De Gaetano, C. (2021). Google Images, climate change, and the disappearance of humans. *Revista Diseña*, 19: doi.org/10.7764/disena.19.Article.3.

Pearce, W., Özkula, S. M., Greene, A. K., Teeling, L., Bansard, J. S., Omena, J. J. & Rabello, E. T. (2020). Visual cross-platform analysis: digital methods to research social media images. *Information, Communication & Society*, 23(2), 161–80: https://doi.org/10.1080/1369118X.2018.1486871.

Perez, H. & Tah, J. H. M. (2020). Improving the accuracy of convolutional neural networks by identifying and removing outlier images in datasets using t-SNE. *Mathematics*, 8(5), 662: doi.org/10.3390/math8050662.

pharmapsychotic (2023). CLIP Interrogator – A Hugging Face space by pharma. Retrieved from https://huggingface.co/spaces/pharma/CLIP-Interrogator.

Phillips, W. & Milner, R. M. (2017). *The Ambivalent Internet: Mischief, Oddity, and Antagonism Online*. Cambridge, UK and Malden, MA: Polity.

Pichon, L. C., Teti, M. & Brown, L. L. (2022). Triggers or prompts? When methods resurface unsafe memories and the value of trauma-informed photovoice research practices. *International Journal of Qualitative Methods*, 21: https://doi.org/10.1177/16094069221113979.

Pink, S. (2012). *Advances in Visual Methodology*. London: SAGE Publications: https://doi.org/10.4135/9781446250921.

Prosser, J. (ed.) (1998). *Image-Based Research: A Sourcebook for Qualitative Researchers*. London: Falmer Press.

Puig de la Bellacasa, M. (2011). Matters of care in technoscience: assembling neglected things. *Social Studies of Science*, 4(1), 85–106: https://doi.org/10.1177/0306312710380301.

Puig de la Bellacasa, M. (2017). *Matters of Care: Speculative Ethics in More than Human Worlds*. Minneapolis: University of Minnesota Press.

Pulliam-Moore, C. (2023, 13 July). SAG-AFTRA goes on strike at midnight tonight. Retrieved from The Verge website: www.theverge.com/2023/7/13/23792030/sag-aftra-strike-amptp.

Rabello, E. T., Gommeh, E., Benedetti, A., Valerio-Ureña, G. & Metze, T. (2021). Mapping online visuals of shale gas controversy: a digital methods approach. *Information, Communication & Society*, 1–18: https://doi.org/10.1080/1369118X.2021.1934064.

Rambukkana, N. (ed.) (2015). *Hashtag Publics: The Power and Politics of Discursive Networks*. New York: Peter Lang.

Rawsthorn, A. (2022). *Design as an Attitude*. Zurich: JRP Ringler.

Razsa, M. J. (2014). Beyond 'riot porn': protest video and the production of unruly subjects. *Ethnos*, 79(4), 496–524: https://doi.org/10.1080/00141844.2013.778309.

Ricci, D., Calibro, Evennou, D., & Verjat, B. (2021). Developing online images: from visual traces to public voices. *Revista Diseña*, 19: doi.org/10.7764/disena.19.Article.2.

Ricci, D., Colombo, G., Meunier, A. & Brilli, A. (2017, June). Designing digital methods to monitor and inform urban policy: the case of Paris and its Urban Nature initiative. Presented at the International Conference on Public Policy (ICPP3), Singapore.

Retrieved from https://hal-sciencespo.archives-ouvertes.fr/hal -01903809v2/document.

Rieder, B., Matamoros-Fernández, A. & Coromina, Ò. (2018). From ranking algorithms to 'ranking cultures': investigating the modulation of visibility in YouTube search results. *Convergence: The International Journal of Research into New Media Technologies*, 24(1), 50–68: https://doi.org/10.1177/1354856517736982.

Rogers, R. (2013). *Digital Methods*. Cambridge, MA: The MIT Press.

Rogers, R. (2017a). Foundations of digital methods: query design. In M. T. Schäfer & K. van Es (eds.), *The Datafied Society* (pp. 75–94). Amsterdam University Press: https://doi.org/10.1515 /9789048531011-008.

Rogers, R. (2017b). Memes as platform content. The history of the meme as object of study is one of its gradual denaturalization. Digital Methods Initiative. Retrieved from Digital Methods Initiative website: https://wiki.digitalmethods.net/pub/Dmi/WinterSchool2017 /DMIR_2016_worksheet7_platform_content.pdf.

Rogers, R. (2018a). Aestheticizing Google critique: a 20-year retro-spective. *Big Data & Society*, 5(1): https://doi.org/10.1177 /2053951718768626.

Rogers, R. (2018b). Digital methods for cross-platform analysis. In J. Burgess, A. Marwick, & T. Poell (eds.), *The SAGE Handbook of Social Media* (pp. 91–108). London: SAGE Publications: https://doi .org/ 10.4135/9781473984066.n6.

Rogers, R. (2018c). Otherwise engaged: social media from vanity metrics to critical analytics. *International Journal Of Communication*, 12, 24.

Rogers, R. (2019). *Doing Digital Methods*. Thousand Oaks, CA: SAGE Publications.

Rogers, R. (2021). Visual media analysis for Instagram and other online platforms. *Big Data & Society*, 8(1): https://doi.org/10.1177 /20539517211022370.

Rogers, R. & Sendijarevic, E. (2012). Neutral or national point of view? A comparison of Srebrenica articles across Wikipedia's language versions. Presented at Wikipedia Academy: Research and Free Knowledge: June 29 – July 1, 2012, Berlin. Retrieved from http://wikipediaacademy.de/2012/w/images/8/89/3_Paper_Richard _Rogers_Emina_Sendijarevic.pdf.

Rombach, R. & Esser, P. (2022, June). Stable Diffusion v1-4 model card. Retrieved from https://huggingface.co/CompVis/stable-diffusion-v1-4.

Rose, G. (2016). *Visual Methodologies: An Introduction to Researching with Visual Materials* (4th Edition). London: SAGE Publications.

Rose, J. (2022, 3 November). This tool lets anyone see the bias in AI image generators. Retrieved from Vice website: www.vice.com

/en/article/bvm35w/this-tool-lets-anyone-see-the-bias-in-ai-image
-generators.

Ruscha, E. (1966). Every building on the Sunset Strip. MOMA. Retrieved from www.moma.org/collection/works/146931.

Saenko, K. (2023, 23 May). Is generative AI bad for the environment? A computer scientist explains the carbon footprint of ChatGPT and its cousins. Retrieved from The Conversation website: http://theconversation.com/is-generative-ai-bad-for-the-environment -a-computer-scientist-explains-the-carbon-footprint-of-chatgpt-and -its-cousins-204096.

Salvaggio, E. (2022, 2 October). How to read an AI image [Substack newsletter]. Retrieved from Cybernetic Forests website: https://cyberneticforests.substack.com/p/how-to-read-an-ai-image.

Sánchez-Querubín, N. (2020). Illness online: popular, tagged, and ranked bodies (doctoral dissertation). University of Amsterdam. Retrieved from https://hdl.handle.net/11245.1/23bcb1e2-6eca-4cf4 -9c65-9a4c58c0dc09.

Sandvig, C., Hamilton, K., Karahalios, K. & Langbort, C. (2014, 27 May). Auditing algorithms: research methods for detecting discrimination on internet platforms. Presented at the 64th Annual Meeting of the International Communication Association, Seattle, WA.

Sassoon, J. (2004). Photographic materiality in the age of digital reproduction. In E. Edwards & J. Hart (eds.), *Photographs Objects Histories: on the Materiality of Images* (pp. 186–202). London: Routledge.

Schmidt, F. & Schmieg, S. (n.d.). Prompt battle. Retrieved from Prompt Battle website: https://promptbattle.com.

Schwarzenegger, A. @Schwarzenegger (2017, 13 November). Look what I found at #COP23 while I was fighting for clean air and green energy, @EmmanuelMacron. I'll see you next month, my friend. #MakeOurPlanetGreatAgain https://t.co/qRYdGyBA6F. Twitter. Retrieved from Twitter website: https://twitter.com/Schwarzenegger /status/930058205115363329.

Screen Walks (director). (2022). Screen walk with the Prompt Battle team. Online video interview, retrieved from www.youtube.com /watch?v=mCHAamgZRnQ.

Scuderi, M. (2014). Philippe Rahm architectes: atmosfere costruite l'architettura come design meteorologico. Postmedia.

Shifman, L. (2014). *Memes in Digital Culture*. Cambridge, MA: MIT Press.

Sinders, C. (2017). Feminist data set. University of Denver. Retrieved from University of Denver website: https://carolinesinders.com/wp -content/uploads/2020/05/Feminist-Data-Set-Final-Draft-2020-0526 .pdf.

Sinders, C. (2018). Dear [Redacted], designing for transparency.

Presented at the Digital Methods Initiative summer school, University of Amsterdam.

Sinders, C. (2020). Feminist data set. Available at https://carolinesinders.com/wp-content/uploads/2020/05/Feminist-Data-Set-Final-Draft-2020-0526.pdf.

Smyth, T. & Dimond, J. (2014). Anti-oppressive design. *Interactions*, 21(6), 68–71: https://doi.org/10.1145/2668969.

Snyder, J. (2017). Vernacular visualization practices in a citizen science project. In *Proceedings of the 2017 ACM Conference on Computer Supported Cooperative Work and Social Computing* (pp. 2097–111). Portland, OR: ACM: https://doi.org/10.1145/2998181.2998239.

Spielkamp, M. (2017). Inspecting algorithms for bias. Retrieved from MIT Technology Review website: www.technologyreview.com/2017/06/12/105804/inspecting-algorithms-for-bias.

Stable Diffusion (2023, April). Stable Diffusion web UI wiki – features. Retrieved from GitHub website: https://github.com/AUTOMATIC1111/stable-diffusion-webui/wiki/Features.

Stable Diffusion Art. (2023a, 5 January). How does negative prompt work? Retrieved from https://stable-diffusion-art.com/how-negative-prompt-work.

Stable Diffusion Art. (2023b, 8 February). Stable Diffusion prompt: a definitive guide. Retrieved from https://stable-diffusion-art.com/prompt-guide.

Stanley-Becker, I. & Nix, N. (2023, 24 March). Fake images of Trump arrest show 'giant step' for AI's disruptive power. *Washington Post*. Retrieved from www.washingtonpost.com/politics/2023/03/22/trump-arrest-deepfakes.

Stefaner, M. (2018). Multiplicity: a collective photographic city portrait. Retrieved from https://truth-and-beauty.net/projects/multiplicity.

Stepnik, A., Martin, A., Benedetti, A., Karsgaard, C., Yee Ting Ng, C., Major, D., Garcia-Mingo, E., Geboers, M., Granzotto, F., Gullal, G. M., Krol, J., Kuculo, T., van Vliet, L. (2020). Black Squares as (in)authentic behavior: displays of solidarity on Twitter, Instagram and Facebook. Retrieved from https://wiki.digitalmethods.net/Dmi/SummerSchool2020BlackSquares.

Steyerl, H. (2009). In defense of the poor image. Retrieved from e-flux website: www.e-flux.com/journal/10/61362/in-defense-of-the-poor-image.

Steyerl, H. (2013, November). Too much world: is the internet dead? Retrieved from e-flux website: www.e-flux.com/journal/49/60004/too-much-world-is-the-internet-dead.

Steyerl, H. (2023). Mean Images. *New Left Review*, 140/141, 82–97.

Strickland, E. (2022, 14 July). DALL-E 2's failures are the most interesting thing about it. *IEEE Spectrum*. Retrieved from https://spectrum.ieee.org/openai-dall-e-2.

Sze, S. (2018). Sarah Sze: infinite generation (interviewer: L. Neri). Retrieved from https://gagosian.com/quarterly/2019/10/08/interview-sarah-sze-infinite-generation.

TEDxAmsterdam Women (2023). MissJourney AI. Retrieved from MissJourney website: https://missjourney.ai.

The Economist (2022, June). How a computer designed this week's cover. *The Economist*. Retrieved from www.economist.com/news/2022/06/11/how-a-computer-designed-this-weeks-cover.

The New York Times – The Learning Network (n.d.). Student opinion. *The New York Times*. Retrieved from www.nytimes.com/column/learning-student-opinion.

Thelwall, M., Goriunova, O., Vis, F., Faulkner, S., Burns, A., Aulich, J., Mas-Bleda, A., Stuart, E. & D'Orazio, F. (2016). Chatting through pictures? A classification of images tweeted in one week in the UK and USA. *Journal of the Association for Information Science and Technology*, 67(11), 2575–86: doi.org/10.1002/asi.23620.

Tiidenberg, K. & Baym, N. K. (2017). Learn it, buy it, work it: intensive pregnancy on Instagram. *Social Media + Society*, 3(1): doi.org/10.1177/2056305116685108.

Traylor, J. (2022, 27 July). No quick fix: how OpenAI's DALL·E 2 illustrated the challenges of bias in AI. Retrieved from *NBC News* website: www.nbcnews.com/tech/tech-news/no-quick-fix-openais-dalle-2-illustrated-challenges-bias-ai-rcna39918.

Tufte, E. R. (2001). *The Visual Display of Quantitative Information* (2nd edition). Cheshire, CT: Graphics Press.

Umbrico, P. (2013). Sunset portraits. Retrieved from www.penelopeumbrico.net/index.php/project/sunset-portraits.

Valdivia, A. N. & Manovich, L. (2012). Media visualization. In A. N. Valdivia (ed.), *The International Encyclopedia of Media Studies*. Oxford: Blackwell Publishing Ltd: doi.org/10.1002/9781444361506.wbiems144.

Van Leeuwen, T. & Jewitt, C. (eds.) (2001). *Handbook of Visual Analysis*. London: SAGE Publications.

Venturini, T., Jacomy, M. & Pereira, D. (2014). Visual network analysis. *MediaLab Working Papers*.

Venturini, T., Jacomy, M. & Jensen, P. (2021). What do we see when we look at networks: visual network analysis, relational ambiguity, and force-directed layouts. *Big Data & Society*, 8(1): https://doi.org/10.1177/20539517211018488.

Versluis, A. & Uyttenbroek, E. (2002). *Exactitudes*. Rotterdam: 010 Publishers.

Viégas, F. B. & Wattenberg, M. (2008). Tag clouds and the case for

vernacular visualization. *Interactions*, 15(4), 49–52: https://doi.org
/10.1145/1374489.1374501.

Vincent, J. (2018, 12 January). Google 'fixed' its racist algorithm by
removing gorillas from its image-labeling tech. Retrieved from
The Verge website: www.theverge.com/2018/1/12/16882408/google
-racist-gorillas-photo-recognition-algorithm-ai.

Vincent, J. (2022, 15 September). Anyone can use this AI art generator
– that's the risk. Retrieved from The Verge website: www.theverge
.com/2022/9/15/23340673/ai-image-generation-stable-diffusion
-explained-ethics-copyright-data.

Vogelaar, C. (2017). *Gazeplots*. Retrieved from https://coralievogelaar
.com/Gazeplot.

Wadhwani, D. (2023, 21 March). Bringing generative AI into Creative
Cloud with Adobe Firefly. Retrieved from Adobe Blog website:
https://blog.adobe.com/en/publish/2023/03/21/bringing-gen-ai-to
-creative-cloud-adobe-firefly.

Weinberg, A. (2019). Stop sharing those viral photos of the Amazon
burning. Retrieved from Mother Jones website: www.motherjones
.com/environment/2019/08/viral-photos-amazon-fire-fake-macron.

Zhu, X., Goldberg, A. B., Eldawy, M., Dyer, C. R. & Strock, B. (2007).
A text-to-picture synthesis system for augmenting communication.
In *Proceedings of the 22nd National Conference on Artificial
Intelligence, July 22–26, 2007, Vancouver, British Columbia, Canada*
(vol. II, pp. 1590–5).

Zylinska, J. (2017). *Nonhuman Photography*. Cambridge, MA: MIT
Press.

Index

Page numbers in *italics* refer to figures.